D0104473

ISBN 978-0-9842315-0-8

Designed by Fluid Communications, Inc.

Printed and bound in the United States of America.

THRU THE BIBLE

Briefing

THE

Bible

A trusted tool to get you started
studying every book of the Bible

DR. J. VERNON MCGEE

TABLE OF CONTENTS

OLD TESTAMENT

NEW TESTAMENT

HOW TO USE THIS BOOK

Reading the Bible is one of the most important things we can ever do.

You likely believe that, considering you hold in your hand a book devoted to walking you through the pages of the Bible, book by book. Dr. J. Vernon McGee, the author of these pages, certainly believed that. But why? *What makes the Bible so important? And how can I make reading it and living by it a pattern of my life?* Those are the important questions we must answer before we dive in.

WHAT MAKES THE BIBLE SO IMPORTANT?

The books of your Bible—down to the very words written—are God's thoughts; they are God's words. *In your hands.* If you believe that, the Bible becomes more than ink on a page but something supernatural. God, using human authors in various life situations, wrote it for one purpose: To introduce you to Himself. The God who spoke light out of darkness wants to speak truth into your mind and heart. That truth will lead you to His Son, Jesus— whom to know is life eternal (John 17:3).

And that's just the beginning. Through His Word, the Spirit of God awakens us to new life. He frees us from the chains of sin. He comforts the depressed, inspires the discouraged, guides the confused. He empowers us to live by faith—because faith comes by hearing the Word of God (Romans 10:17).

HOW CAN I MAKE THIS TREASURE A PART OF MY LIFE?

Following the Lord takes commitment and effort. But everyone who makes God's Word a priority in their lives will testify that it's a discipline that God uses to transform their lives. Whether you're a beginner or a veteran at Bible study, you'll benefit from these seven practices, fully discussed in Dr. McGee's *Guidelines to Understanding Scripture*. These steps will help you make God's Word your lifelong companion:

1 – Begin with prayer	5 – Read what others have written on the Bible
2 – Read the Bible	
3 – Study the Bible	6 – Obey the Bible
4 – Meditate on the Bible	7 – Pass it on to others

The content that follows in this book, *Briefing the Bible*, will be especially helpful in reading and studying each book of the Bible. Before diving into each book, review the outline, read over Dr. McGee's notes, and you'll be better equipped to understand God's message for you.

OF COURSE, WHEN YOU'RE READY TO GO DEEPER, WE WANT TO HELP.

- Download the complete versions of Dr. McGee's Notes & Outlines for each book of the Bible at TTB.org/notes.
- Dr. McGee's detailed lessons, often verse by verse, are also available to you online at TTB.org/study.
- Or even easier, go to TTB.org/romans (or whatever book you're studying). There you'll find study helps, the audio to every lesson, and more.

When you commit yourself to the study of God's Word, you are on the journey of a lifetime. THRU the BIBLE is honored to be your companion on your adventure.

SHARE THIS BLESSING WITH OTHERS! Purchase additional copies of *Briefing the Bible*—or download a free digital copy—at TTB.org/briefing.

GUIDELINES TO UNDERSTANDING SCRIPTURE

INTRODUCTION

IS THE BIBLE IMPORTANT?

The Bible is probably the most maligned book that ever has been written. It has been attacked as no other book has ever been attacked. Yet it has ministered and does minister to literally millions of people around the globe, and it has been doing this now for several thousand years. A book of this nature and with this tremendous impact upon the human family certainly deserves the intelligent consideration of men and women.

Sir Walter Scott, on his deathbed, asked Lockhart to read to him. Puzzled, as he scanned the shelf of books that Walter Scott had written, he asked, "What book shall I read?" And Sir Walter replied, "Why do you ask that question? There is but one book; bring the Bible." There is only one book for any man who is dying, but it is also *the* book for any man who is living. A great many folk do not get interested in the Bible until they get to the end of their lives or until they get into a great deal of difficulty. While it is wonderful to have a book in which you can find comfort in a time like that, it is also a book for you to *live*—in the full vigor of life. It is a book to face life with today, and it's the book which furnishes the only sure route through this world and on into the next world. It is the only book that can enable us to meet the emergencies and cushion the shocks that come to us in life. The Bible is different from any other book.

That this book has influenced great men who, in turn, have influenced the world is evident. Let me share with you some quotations.

There was an African prince who came to England and was presented to Her Majesty Queen Victoria. This prince asked a very significant question, "What is the secret of England's greatness?" The queen got a beautifully bound copy of the Bible and presented it to the prince with this statement: "This is the secret of England's greatness." I wonder, friend, if England's decline to a second-rate and then third-rate nation may be tied up in the fact that England has gotten away from the Word of God.

Gladstone, statesman, prime minister, probably one of the greatest legal minds Britain ever produced, said, "Talk about the questions of the day! There is but one question, and that is the gospel. That can and will correct everything. I am glad to say that about all the men at the top in Great Britain are Christians." That was way back in the 1800s. Gladstone continued, "I have been in public position 58 years, all but 11 of them in the Cabinet of the British Government, and during those 47 years have been associated with 60 of the masterminds of the century, and all but five of the 60 were Christians." I personally think that part of the problems we are having in the world today is that we have too few Christians at the top, too few who are acquainted with the Word of God.

Michael Faraday, perhaps the greatest scientific experimenter back in the 1800s, said, "But why will people go astray, when they have this blessed book of God to guide them?" Sir Isaac Newton, a scientist in the preceding century, said, "If the Bible is true, the time is coming when men shall travel at 50 miles an hour." In response Voltaire, the French skeptic, commented, "Poor Isaac. He was in his dotage when he made that prophecy. It only shows what Bible study will do to an otherwise scientific mind."

It might be interesting to note what some of our early Presidents had to say about the Bible. John Adams, our second President, said, "I have examined all [that is, all of Scripture] as well as my narrow sphere, my straightened means, and my busy life will allow me, and the result is that the Bible is the best book in the world. It contains more of my little philosophy than all the libraries I have seen, and such parts of it I cannot reconcile to my little philosophy I postpone for future investigation." Then President John Quincy Adams said, "I speak as a man of the world to men of the world; and I say to you: search the Scriptures. The Bible is the book above all others to be read at all ages and in all conditions of human life; not to be read once or twice through and then laid aside, but to be read in small portions every day." And the Presidents back in those days, who made our nation great, did not get us into foreign wars and were able to solve the problems of the streets. Someone may counter, "But the problems weren't as complicated then as they are now." They were for that day, friend.

Not only England but also the United States has gotten away from the Word of God. And the farther we get, the more complicated our problems become. Right now there are men and women in positions of authority in this land who are saying that there is no solution to our problems. That is the reason I am teaching the Word of God in its entirety—I believe it is the only solution. And, frankly, friend, we had better get back to it.

Another President, Thomas Jefferson, said this about the Bible: "I have always said, and always will say, that the studious perusal of the Sacred Volume will make better citizens, better husbands, and better fathers." This is something to think over today when our citizens are burning down the cities in which they live and when divorce is running rife.

It was Daniel Webster who made this statement: "If there be anything in my style or thoughts to be commended, the credit is due to my kind parents for instilling into my mind an early love of the Scriptures." What about you today, Christian parent? Are you making a Daniel Webster in your home or a little rebel? Webster also made this statement: "I have read it [the Bible] through many times. I now make a practice of going through it once a year. It is the book of all others for lawyers as well as divines. I pity the man who cannot find in it a rich supply of thought and rules for conduct."

THE BOOK OF BOOKS

Born in the East and clothed in Oriental form and imagery, the Bible walks the ways of all the world with familiar feet, and enters land after land to find its own everywhere. It has learned to speak in hundreds of languages to the heart of man. It comes into the palace to tell the monarch that he is a servant of the Most High, and into the cottage to assure the peasant that he is a son of God. Children listen to its stories with wonder and delight, and wise men ponder them as parables of life. It has a word of peace for the time of peril, a word of comfort for the time of calamity, a word of light for the hour of darkness. Its oracles are repeated in the assembly of the people, and its counsels whispered in the ear of the lonely. The wicked and the proud tremble at its warnings, but to the wounded and the penitent it has a mother's voice. The wilderness and the solitary place have been made glad by it, and the fire on the hearth has lit the reading of its well-worn pages. It has woven itself into our dearest dreams; so that love, friendship, sympathy and devotion, memory and hope put on the beautiful garments of its treasured speech, breathing of frankincense and myrrh.

—Henry van Dyke

IN WHAT WAY IS THE BIBLE UNIQUE?

In many ways the Bible is a most unusual book. For instance, it has a dual authorship. In other words, God is the Author of the Bible, and in another sense man is the author of the Bible. Actually, the Bible was written by about 40 authors over a period of approximately 1500 years. Some of these men never even heard of the others, and there was no collusion among the 40. Two or three of them could have gotten together, but the others could not have known each other. And yet they have presented a book that has the most marvelous continuity of any book that has ever been written. Also, it is without error. Each author expressed his own feelings in his own generation. Each had his limitations and made his mistakes—poor old Moses made mistakes, but when he was writing the Pentateuch, somehow or other no mistakes got in there. You see, it is a human book and yet it is a God-book.

It is a very human book, written by men from all walks of life, prince and pauper, the highly intellectual and the very simple. For example, Dr. Luke writes almost classical Greek in a period when the Koine Greek was popular. His Greek is marvelous! But Simon Peter, the fisherman, wrote some Greek also. His is not so good, but God the Holy Spirit used both of these men. He let them express exactly their thoughts, their feelings, and yet through that method the Spirit of God was able to overrule in such a way that God said exactly what He wanted to say. That's the wonder of the book, the Bible.

It is a God-book. In the Bible God says 2500 times, "God said ... the Lord has said ... thus saith the Lord," etc. God has made it very clear that He is speaking through this book. It is a book that can communicate life to you. You can even become a child of God, begotten "not by corruptible seed, but by incorruptible, by the Word of God that liveth and abideth forever." It is God's communication to man. And if God spoke out of heaven right now, He would just repeat Himself because He has said all that He wants to say to this generation. And, by the way, He didn't learn anything when He read the morning paper. When man went to the moon, he didn't discover anything that God didn't already know when He gave us the Bible. He is the same God who created this universe that we are in today.

The Bible is both divine and human. In a way it is like my Lord who walked down here and grew weary and sat down at a well. Although He was God, He was man. He talked with people down here and communicated with them. This is a book that communicates. It speaks to mankind today. The Bible is for men as they are.

> *The Bible is a corridor between two eternities down which walks the Christ of God; His invisible steps echo through the Old Testament, but we meet Him face to face in the throne room of the New; and it is through that Christ alone, crucified for me, that I have found forgiveness for sins and life eternal. The Old Testament is summed up in the word Christ; the New Testament is summed up in the word Jesus; and the summary of the whole Bible is that Jesus is the Christ.*

> —Bishop Pollock

HOW DO YOU KNOW THE BIBLE IS FROM GOD?

How do you know the Bible is the Word of God? This is a good question, and it should be asked and answered.

1 PRESERVATION—One of the objective proofs, one of the external proofs, has been the marvelous preservation of the Bible. There was a king of old—we read about him in the book of Jeremiah— who, when the Word was sent to him, took a penknife and cut it to pieces. But it was rewritten, and we have that Word today. Down through the centuries there have been a great many Bible burnings. Today there's a great deal of antagonism toward the Bible. In our country today it is not being burned because we think that we are too civilized for such behavior. The way they try to get rid of it

is just to outlaw it in our schools and in many other places. (Yet we talk about our freedom of religion and freedom of speech.) In spite of all the attacks that have been made upon the Bible, it still today exists, and, of course, it's one of the best sellers. For many years it was *the* best seller, but it's not today. I regret to have to say that, but it is true. And that is certainly a commentary on our contemporary society. It reveals that the Bible is not really occupying the place that it once did in the history and in the life of this nation. Yet, I think the amazing preservation of the Word of God is worthy of consideration.

2 ARCHAEOLOGY–Another way in which we can know the Bible is the Word of God is through archaeology. The spade of the archaeologist has turned up many things that have proven that it is the Word of God. For instance, there were those who for many years denied the Mosaic authorship of the Pentateuch on the basis that writing was not in existence in Moses' day. You haven't heard anybody advance that theory recently, have you? Well, of course not. For years the spade of the archaeologist has turned up again and again evidence of the validity of the Bible. The city of Jericho and the walls that fell down is one example. Now there has been some argument between Miss Kathleen Kenyon and John Garstang relative to specifics, but it's well established that the walls fell down, and I'll let them debate about the time and all that sort of thing. The Word of God has been substantiated there, and in many other ways archaeology has demonstrated the accuracy of the Bible. Many of the manuscripts that have been found do that also. It's quite interesting that when the Isaiah scrolls, the Dead Sea scrolls, were found, the liberal leaped at that because he thought he had found an argument that would discredit the Bible. However, the scrolls have not discredited the Bible, and it seems that the liberal has lost a great deal of interest in them. This is a field into which you might do some research, as I cannot go to any great length in this brief study.

3 FULFILLED PROPHECY–If I were asked today if I had just one thing to suggest that would be a conclusive proof that the Bible is the Word of God, do you know what I would suggest? I would suggest fulfilled prophecy. Fulfilled prophecy is the one proof that you can't escape, you can't get around. And the Bible is filled with fulfilled prophecy. One-fourth of the Scripture, when it was written, was prophetic; that is, it announced things that were to take place in the future. A great deal of that—in fact, a great deal more than people imagine—has already been fulfilled. We could turn to many places where prophecy has been fulfilled exactly. We find that there were many local situations that were fulfilled even in the day of the prophet. For example, Micaiah was the prophet who told Ahab that if he went out to battle as he planned, he would lose the battle and would be killed. However, Ahab's false prophets had told him he'd have a victory and would return as a victorious king. Because he didn't like what Micaiah said, Ahab ordered him locked up and fed bread and water, and he would take care of him when he got back. But Micaiah shot back the last word, "If you come back at all, the Lord hasn't spoken by me." Well, evidently the Lord had spoken by him because Ahab didn't come back. He was killed in the battle, and his army was defeated. He had even disguised himself so that there would be no danger of his losing his life. But an enemy soldier, the Scripture says, pulled his bow at a venture; that is, when the battle was about over, he had just one arrow left in his quiver; he put it in place and shot, not really aiming at anything. But, you know, that arrow had old Ahab's name on it, and it found him. It went right to its mark. Why? Because Micaiah had made an accurate prophecy (see 1 Kings 22).

On another occasion, the prophet Isaiah said that the invading Assyrian army wouldn't shoot an arrow into the city of Jerusalem (see 2 Kings 19:32). Well, now, that's interesting. Micaiah's prophecy was fulfilled because a soldier shot an arrow by chance, pulled his bow at a venture. Wouldn't you think that among 200,000 soldiers—that "great host"—perhaps one might be trigger-happy and would pull his bow at a venture and let an arrow fly over the wall of Jerusalem? Well, he didn't. If the enemy had shot an arrow inside that city, they could be sure that Isaiah was not God's prophet. But he was, as was proven by this local fulfillment of his prophecy. But Isaiah also said a virgin would bring forth a child, and that was 700 years before it was literally fulfilled. And then, if you want a final proof, there were over 300 prophecies concerning the first coming of Christ which were all literally fulfilled. As Jesus Christ was hanging there on the cross and dying, there was one prophecy recorded in the Old Testament that had not been fulfilled. It was, "They gave me vinegar to drink" (Psalm 69:21). Jesus said, "I thirst," and the enemy himself went and fulfilled prophecy (see John 19:28-30). It's a most amazing thing. Men can't guess like that. It has been rather amusing to watch the weatherman. During the summer season in Southern California he does fine, but when we get to the change of seasons—well, your guess is as good as his. In the nation Israel, a prophet had to be accurate. If he was not accurate, he was to be put to death as a false prophet. God told His people that they would be able to distinguish a false prophet from a true prophet. A true prophet must first speak into a local situation, which Isaiah did. When that prophecy came to pass, they would know they could trust him to speak concerning the future, as Isaiah did. We can look back now and know that it was fulfilled.

There are so many other prophecies. Tyre and Sidon are over there today exactly as God's Word said 2500 years ago they would be. Egypt today is in the exact position God said it would be in. All of these are amazing, friend, and fulfilled prophecy is one of the greatest proofs that the Bible is indeed the Word of God. You see, men just can't be that accurate. Men can't guess like that—even the weatherman misses it.

Let me show you that, according to mathematical law of problematical conjecture, man could never, never prophesy. Suppose that right now I would make a prophecy. Just by way of illustration, suppose I'd say that wherever you are it's going to rain tomorrow. I'd have a 50% change of being right because it'll do one of the two. For some of you it would probably be accurate. For others it would not. But suppose that I add to that and say it would start raining tomorrow morning at nine o'clock. That would be another uncertain element. I had a 50-50 chance of being right at first; now I have a 25% chance. Every uncertain element that is added reduces by 50% the chance of my being right—the law of problematical conjecture. Now suppose that I not only say that it's going to start raining at nine o'clock, but I also say it'll stop raining at two o'clock. Well, believe me, friend, that has reduced my chances now another 50% which brings it down to 12%. Can you imagine my chance of being right now? But suppose I add 300 uncertain elements. There's not a ghost of a chance of being accurate. I just couldn't hit it—it would be impossible. Yet the Word of God hit it, my friend. It is accurate. The Bible has moved into that area of absolute impossibility, and that to me is absolute proof that it is the Word of God. There is nothing to compare to it at all. I have given very few examples of fulfilled prophecy, but there is in the Word of God prophecy after prophecy, and they have been fulfilled—literally fulfilled. And by the way, I would think that that indicates the method in which prophecy for the future is yet to be fulfilled.

4 TRANSFORMED LIVES—I offer two final reasons as proof that the Bible is the Word of God. One is the transformed lives of believers today. I have seen what the Word of God can do in the lives of men and women. I'm thinking right now of a man in Oakland, California, who listened to my Bible-teaching program. I know this man. I'm not going into detail in his life at all, but he probably had as many problems, as many hang-ups, and he was in as much sin as any man that I know anything about. And this man began to listen to the radio program. I hear of people who just hear the gospel once and are converted. I think it's possible and that it's wonderful. But this man listened to it week after week, and he became antagonistic. He became angry. Later he said to me, "If I could have gotten to you when you were teaching the Epistle to the Romans and told me that I was a sinner, I would have hit you in the nose," and frankly, friend, I think he could have done it. He's much bigger and much younger than I am. I'm glad he couldn't get to me. Finally, this man turned to Christ. May I say to you, it has been wonderful to see what God has done in his life. Again and again and again this testimony could be multiplied. Young and old have found purpose and fulfillment in life, marriages have been saved, families reunited, individuals have been freed from alcoholism and drug addiction. Folk have had their lives transformed by coming to Christ. Now let me give you a reason. When I finished seminary, I was a preacher who majored in the realm of the defense of the gospel, and I attempted to defend the Bible. In fact, I think every message I gave entered into that area. I felt if I could just get enough answers to the questions that people have for not believing the Bible that they would believe. But I found out that the worst thing I could do was to whip a man down intellectually. The minute I did that, I made an enemy and never could win him for the Lord. So I moved out of the realm of apologetics and into another area of just giving out the Word of God as simply as I could. Only the Bible can turn a sinner into a saint.

5 SPIRIT OF GOD MADE IT REAL—Another reason that I've moved out of the realm of apologetics is because there has been a certain development in my own life. I have reached the place today where I not only believe that the Bible is the Word of God, I *know* it's the Word of God. And I know it's the Word of God because the Spirit of God has made it real to my own heart and my own life. That is the thing that Paul talked to the Colossians about. He prayed that they "might be filled with the knowledge of his will in all wisdom and spiritual understanding." I also want this, because I found out that the Spirit of God can confirm these things to your heart and that you don't need archaeology or anything else to prove that the Bible is God's Word. A young preacher said to me some time ago, "Dr. McGee, isn't it wonderful that they have discovered this," and he mentioned something in particular. And I said, "Well, I don't see anything to be excited about." He was greatly disappointed and even chagrined that I was so far away from it that I did not respond enthusiastically. "Why, what do you mean?" he asked. "Is it possible that this hasn't impressed you?" Well, I answered him this way, "I already knew it was the Word of God long before the spade of the archaeologist turned that up." He asked how I knew it, and I said, "The Spirit of God has been making it real to my own heart." I trust that the Spirit of God is going to make the Word of God not only real to you to incorporate into your living, but that He is also going to give you that assurance that you can say, "I know that it's the Word of God."

> Whence but from Heaven, could men unskilled in arts,
> In several ages born, in several parts,
> Weave such agreeing truths, or how, or why,
> Should all conspire to cheat us with a lie?
> Unasked their pains, ungrateful their advice,
> Starving their gain, and martyrdom their price.
>
> —John Dryden

WHAT DO YOU MEAN BY REVELATION? INSPIRATION? ILLUMINATION? INTERPRETATION?

Revelation means that God has spoken and that God has communicated to man. *Inspiration* guarantees the revelation of God. *Illumination* has to do with the Spirit of God being the Teacher— He communicates. *Interpretation* has to do with the interpretation that you and I give to the Word of God.

Revelation

Revelation means that God has spoken. "Thus saith the Lord," and its equivalent, occurs over 2500 times. The Lord didn't want you to misunderstand that He had spoken. Notice Hebrews 1:1, 2:

> *God, who at sundry times and in divers manners spake in time past unto the fathers by the prophets, hath in these last days*

spoken unto us by his Son, whom he hath appointed heir of all things, by whom also he made the worlds.

Wherever you will find two persons, endowed with a reasonable degree of intelligence, who harbor the same feelings and desires, who are attracted to each other more or less, you will find communication between them. Persons of like propensities, separated from each other, delight in getting in touch with each other and rejoice in receiving communication from each other. This innate characteristic of the human heart explains the post office department, the telephone, and the telegraph.

Friends communicate with friends. A husband away from home writes to his wife. A boy or girl at school will write home to dad and mom. And ever and anon there travels the scented epistle of a girl to a boy, and then the boy returns an epistle to the girl. All of this is called communication. It is the expression of the heart. The Scripture says, "Deep calls to deep." You will recall the story of Helen Keller. I remember the thrill that came to me when I read the account of this woman, shut out from the world by blindness and deafness, without means of communication; and then a way was opened up so she could communicate—probably better than many of us who can see and hear.

Now, on the basis of all this, I would like to ask you what I believe is a reasonable and certainly an intelligent question: Isn't it reasonable to conclude that God has communicated with His creatures to whom He has committed a certain degree of intelligence and whom He created in His likeness? May I say to you, if we did not have a revelation from God, right now I think that you and I could just wait and He would be speaking to us, because we could expect God to speak to us. You will notice that the writer to the Hebrews says that God in the Old Testament spoke through the prophets, and He now has spoken through Christ. Both the revelation to the prophets in the Old Testament and the revelation of Christ in the New Testament are in the Word of God, of course, and that is the only way we would know about the communication from either one. The Bible has 66 books, and God has spoken to us through them.

This book contains the mind of God, the state of man, the way of salvation, the doom of sinners and the happiness of believers. Its doctrines are holy, its precepts are binding, its histories are true, and its decisions are immutable. Read it to be wise, believe it to be safe and practice it to be holy. It contains light to direct you, food to support you and comfort to cheer you. It is the traveler's map, the pilgrim's staff, the pilot's compass, the soldier's sword and the Christian's character. Here paradise is restored, heaven opened and the gates of hell disclosed. Christ is its grand object, our good is its design and the glory of God its end. It should fill the memory, rule the heart, and guide the feet. Read it slowly, frequently, and prayerfully. It is given you in life and will be opened in the judgment and will be remembered forever. It involves the highest responsibility, will reward the greatest labour, and will condemn all who trifle with its sacred contents.

—Author unknown

Inspiration

This brings us to the second great subject which is *inspiration*. I personally believe in what is known as the plenary verbal inspiration of the Scriptures, which means that the Bible is an authoritative statement and that every word of it is the Word of God to us and for us in this day in which we live. Inspiration guarantees the revelation of God. And that is exactly what this book says. Two men, both Paul writing his last epistle to Timothy and Peter writing his last epistle, had something pretty definite to say about the Bible:

All scripture is given by inspiration of God, and is profitable for doctrine, for reproof, for correction, for instruction in righteousness: that the man of God may be perfect, throughly furnished unto all good works. (2 Timothy 3:16, 17 NSRB)

Notice that *all* Scripture is given by inspiration. The word "inspiration" means God *breathed*. God said through these men, as He said here through Paul, exactly what He wanted to say. He hasn't anything else to add. Peter expresses it this way:

For the prophecy came not in old time by the will of man: but holy men of God spake as they were moved by the Holy Ghost. (2 Peter 1:21)

It is very important to see that these men were moved, as it were, carried along, by the Holy Spirit of God. It was Bishop Westcott who said: "The thoughts are wedded to words as necessarily as the soul is to the body." And Dr. Keiper said, "You can as easily have music without notes, or mathematics without figures, as thoughts without words." It is not the thoughts that are inspired; it's the *words* that are inspired.

There is a little whimsical story of a girl who had taken singing lessons from a very famous teacher. He was present at her recital, and after it was over she was anxious to know his reaction. He didn't come backstage to congratulate her, and she asked a friend, "What did he say?" Her loyal friend answered, "He said that you sang heavenly." She couldn't quite believe that her teacher had said that; so she probed, "Is that *exactly* what he said?" "Well, no, but that is what he meant." The girl insisted, "Tell me the *exact* words that he used." "Well, his exact words were, 'That was an unearthly noise!'" May I say to you, there is a difference between unearthly noise and heavenly sound. Exact words are important.

Believe me, it is the words of Scripture that are inspired—not the thoughts, but the words. For instance, Satan was not inspired to tell a lie, but the Bible records that he told a lie. It's the words that are inspired. And the Lord Jesus said, "It is written," quoting the Word of God in the Old Testament—the men who wrote gave out what God had to say. In Exodus 20:1 Moses wrote: "And God spoke all these words, saying ... ." It was God who did the speaking, and Moses wrote what He said.

Over the years there have been discovered many very excellent manuscripts of the Scriptures. Speaking of the manuscripts in Britain, Sir George Kenyon, the late director and principal librarian of the British Museum, made this statement: "Thanks to these manuscripts, the ordinary reader of the Bible may feel comfortable about the soundness of the text. Apart from a few unimportant verbal alterations, natural in books transcribed by hand, the New Testament, we now feel assured, has come down intact." We can be sure today that we have that which is as close to the autographs as anything possibly can be, and I believe in the verbal plenary inspiration of the autographs—that is, the original manuscripts.

Way back yonder in the second century Irenaeus, one of the church fathers, wrote: "The Scriptures indeed are perfect, forasmuch as they are spoken by the Word of God and by His Spirit." Augustine, living in the fifth century, made this statement, "Let us therefore yield ourselves and bow to the authority of the Holy

Scriptures which can neither err nor deceive." And Spurgeon commented, "I can never doubt the doctrine of plenary verbal inspiration; since I so constantly see, in actual practice, how the very words that God has been pleased to use—a plural instead of a singular—are blessed to the souls of men." *God* speaks in this book to our hearts and to our lives.

Illumination

Illumination means that since you and I have a book, a God-book and a human book, written by men who were expressing their thoughts and while doing this they were writing down the Word of God, only the Spirit of God can teach it to us. Although we can get the facts of the Bible on our own, the Spirit of God will have to open our minds and hearts if we are to understand the spiritual truth that is there.

Paul, writing to the Corinthians, said:

But we speak the wisdom of God in a mystery, even the hidden wisdom, which God ordained before the world unto our glory: which none of the princes of this world knew: for had they known it, they would not have crucified the Lord of glory. But as it is written, Eye hath not seen, nor ear heard, neither have entered into the heart of man, the things which God hath prepared for them that love him. (1 Corinthians 2:7-9)

Now you and I get most of what we know through the eye gate and the ear gate or by reason. Paul tells us here that there are certain things that eye has not seen nor ear heard, certain things that you can't get into your mind at all. Then how in the world are you going to get them?

But God hath revealed them unto us by his Spirit: for the Spirit searcheth all things, yea, the deep things of God. (1 Corinthians 2:10)

Verse 9 sometimes goes to a funeral. The minister implies that the one who has died didn't know too much down here, but now he will know things he did not know before. While that probably is true (we will get quite an education in heaven), that is not what the verse says. Long before you get to the undertaker, there are a lot of things down here that you and I can't learn through natural means. The Holy Spirit has to be our Teacher.

You remember that our Lord inquired of His disciples, "What are men saying about Me?" They said that some were saying one thing and some another. (And today you can get a different answer from almost every person you happen to ask. There are many viewpoints of Him.) Then He asked His disciples:

> ... But whom say ye that I am? And Simon Peter answered and said, Thou art the Christ, the Son of the living God. And Jesus answered and said unto him, Blessed art thou, Simon Bar-jona: for flesh and blood hath not revealed it unto thee, but my Father which is in heaven. (Matthew 16:15-17)

God is the One who revealed the truth to Simon Peter. And today only God can open up the Word of God for us to really understand it.

On the day of the resurrection of the Lord Jesus, He walked down the Emmaus road and joined a couple of men as they walked along. Entering into their conversation, He asked them:

> ... What manner of communications are these that ye have one to another, as ye walk, and are sad? And the one of them, whose name was Cleopas, answering said unto him, Art thou only a stranger in Jerusalem, and hast not known the things which are come to pass there in these days? And he said unto them, What things? And they said unto him, Concerning Jesus of Nazareth, which was a prophet mighty in deed and word before God and all the people: and how the chief priests and our rulers delivered him to be condemned to death, and have crucified him. (Luke 24:17-20)

As you will recall, Jesus had predicted that. And it is interesting to see that written prophecy had been saying it for years. Then they expressed the hope that had been theirs:

> But we trusted that it had been he which should have redeemed Israel: and beside all this, today is the third day since these things were done. (Luke 24:21)

And they went on to tell about what they knew and what the women had reported. "Those who were with us went to the sepulcher ... but Him they saw not." Their hopes had dimmed, and darkness had entered their hearts. Now listen to the Lord Jesus:

... O fools, and slow of heart to believe all that the prophets have spoken: ought not Christ to have suffered these things, and to enter into his glory? And beginning at Moses and all the prophets, he expounded unto them in all the scriptures the things concerning himself. (Luke 24:25-27)

Friend, wouldn't you have loved to have been there that day and heard Him go back in the Old Testament and lift out the Scriptures concerning Himself? And after He finally made Himself known to them as they sat at the evening meal, this is their comment:

... Did not our heart burn within us, while he talked with us by the way, and while he opened to us the scriptures? (Luke 24:32)

You see, we are studying a book that is different from any other book. It is not that I just believe in the inspiration of the Bible, I believe that it is a closed book to you unless the Spirit of God will open your heart and make it real. When Jesus returned to Jerusalem at that time, He continued teaching the disciples:

And he said unto them, These are the words which I spake unto you, while I was yet with you, that all things must be fulfilled, which were written in the law of Moses, and in the prophets, and in the psalms, concerning me. (Luke 24:44)

Notice that He believed Moses wrote the Pentateuch; He believed the prophets spoke of Him and that the Psalms pointed to Him. Now here is the important verse:

Then opened he their understanding, that they might understand the scriptures. (Luke 24:45)

And, friend, if He doesn't open your understanding, you're just not going to get it, that's all. That is the reason we ought to approach this book with great humility of mind, regardless of how high our IQ is or the extent of our education.

Referring back to 1 Corinthians, Paul goes on to say:

Which things also we speak, not in the words which man's wisdom teacheth, but which the Holy Spirit teacheth, comparing spiritual things with spiritual. But the natural man receiveth not the things of the Spirit of God; for they are foolishness unto him, neither can he know them, because they are spiritually discerned. (1 Corinthians 2:13, 14 NSRB)

I am never disturbed when one of these unbelievers, even if he's a preacher, comes along and says he no longer believes the Bible is the Word of God (he never did believe it, to tell the truth) because that's the way he *should* talk. After all, if he is not a believer, he cannot understand it. Mark Twain, who was no believer, said that he was not disturbed by what he did not understand in the Bible. What worried him were the things he *did* understand. There are things an unbeliever can understand, and it's those which cause many to reject the Word of God. It was Pascal who said, "Human knowledge must be understood to be loved, but Divine knowledge must be loved to be understood."

As I leave the subject of illumination let me add this: Only the Spirit of God can open your mind and heart to see and to accept Christ and to trust Him as your Savior. How wonderful! I have always felt as I entered the pulpit how helpless I am because, believe me, Vernon McGee can't convert anyone. But I not only feel weak, I also feel mighty—not mighty in myself, but in the knowledge that the Spirit of God can take my dead words and make them real and living.

Interpretation

Interpretation has to do with the interpretation that you and I give to the Word of God. And this is the reason there are Methodists and Baptists and Presbyterians, this kind of teacher and that kind of teacher—we all have our interpretations. And where there is disagreement, somebody is evidently wrong.

There are several rules that should be followed as we attempt to interpret the Bible.

1 THE OVERALL PURPOSE of the Bible should first be considered. And that is the reason I teach all of it—because I believe you need to have it all before you can come to any dogmatic conclusion concerning any particular verse of Scripture. It is important to take into consideration all verses that are related to that subject.

2 TO WHOM THE SCRIPTURE IS ADDRESSED should next be considered. For instance, way back yonder God said to Joshua, "Arise, go over this Jordan" (Joshua 1:2). When I was over in that land, I crossed the Jordan River, but I didn't cross it to fulfill that Scripture. And I didn't say, "At last I've obeyed the Lord and have crossed over Jordan." No. When I read that verse I know the Lord is talking to

Joshua—but I believe there is a tremendous lesson there for me. All Scripture is not *to* me, but all Scripture is *for* me. That is a good rule to keep in mind.

3 **THE IMMEDIATE CONTEXT** before and after a Scripture should be observed. What is the passage talking about? And what other passages of Scripture deal with the same thing?

4 **DISCOVER WHAT THE ORIGINAL SAYS.** If you do not read Hebrew or Greek, when you read the American Standard Version of 1901 you're right close to what the Lord said. Frankly, I cannot recommend the modern translations, although there are good things in them. I have found that because we are so divided doctrinally, every group that attempts to translate the Bible just naturally injects into the translation their particular viewpoint. Therefore, if the liberal is going to do the translating, you may get a taste of liberalism. If the fundamentalist is going to do the translating, you'll get his bias in certain places. However, the men who did the original English translations were men who believed that the Bible was the Word of God and handled it accordingly. When there were words they could not translate, they simply transliterated them (for instance, *Abba* and *baptizo*). The danger in modern translations is that translation is done in a dogmatic fashion. When you translate, you have to take something out of one language and put it into another language in comparable terms—identical terms if possible. The thing that most of our modern translators are trying to do is to get it into modern speech. And in doing so, they really miss what the original is saying. Personally, I stick by the Authorized King James Version. I feel that The *New Scofield Reference Bible* (NSRB) has made a tremendous step forward in making certain distinctions and corrections that needed to be made in the Authorized Version. I recommend that also, although I still use my old *Scofield Reference Bible*. I know my way around through the book, and, after all, the old scout will follow the old trail. However, the important thing is to attempt to determine the exact words of the original.

5 **INTERPRET THE BIBLE LITERALLY.** The late Dr. David Cooper has stated it well: "When the plain sense of Scripture makes common sense, seek no other sense; therefore, take every word at its primary, ordinary, usual, literal meaning unless the facts of the immediate context, studied in the light of related passages and axiomatic and fundamental truths, indicate clearly otherwise."

GUIDELINES

Open thou mine eyes, that I may behold wondrous things out of thy law. (Psalm 119:18)

There are certain guidelines that each of us should follow relative to the Word of God. I guarantee that if you will follow these guidelines, blessing will come to your heart and life. Certainly there should be these directions in the study of Scripture. Today a bottle of patented medicine, no matter how simple it might be, has directions for the use of it. And any little gadget that you buy in a five-and-ten-cent store has with it directions for its operation. If that is true of the things of this world, certainly the all-important Word of God should have a few directions and instructions on the study of it. I want to mention seven very simple, yet basic, preliminary steps that will be a guide for the study of the Word of God.

1 - Begin with prayer	5 - Read what others have written on the Bible
2 - Read the Bible	
3 - Study the Bible	6 - Obey the Bible
4 - Meditate on the Bible	7 - Pass it on to others

You may want to add to these, but I believe these are basic and primary. Someone has put it in a very brief, cogent manner: "The Bible—know it in your head; stow it in your heart; show it in your life; sow it in the world." That is another way of saying some of the things we are going to present here.

1 BEGIN WITH PRAYER

As we saw when we dealt with the subject of illumination, the Bible differs from other books in that the Holy Spirit alone can open our minds to understand it. You can take up a book on philosophy, and if a man wrote it (and he did), then a man can understand it. The same is true of higher mathematics or any other subject. There is not a book that ever has been written by any man that another man cannot understand. But the Bible is different. The Bible cannot be understood unless the Holy Spirit is the Instructor. And He wants to teach us. The fact of the matter is, our Lord told us,

"He will guide you into all truth" (John 16:13). When we open the Word of God we need to begin with the psalmist's prayer:

> *Open thou mine eyes, that I may behold wondrous things out of thy law.* (Psalm 119:18)

When the psalmist wrote these lines, he had in mind the Mosaic system, of course; but we widen that out to include the 66 books of the Bible and pray today, "Open thou mine eyes, that I may behold wondrous things out of thy *Word*."

When the Apostle Paul was praying for the Ephesians, he did not pray for their health (although he may have at another time), and he did not pray that they might get wealthy (I don't know that he ever did that), but Paul's first prayer for these Ephesians is recorded in his little epistle to them:

> *Wherefore I also, after I heard of your faith in the Lord Jesus, and love unto all the saints, cease not to give thanks for you, making mention of you in my prayers.* (Ephesians 1:15, 16)

Now what would Paul pray for? Here it is:

> *That the God of our Lord Jesus Christ, the Father of glory, may give unto you the spirit of wisdom and revelation in the knowledge of him: the eyes of your understanding being enlightened; that ye may know what is the hope of his calling, and what the riches of the glory of his inheritance in the saints.* (Ephesians 1:17, 18)

Paul's prayer, you see, is that they might have a wisdom and an understanding of the revelation of the knowledge of Him—that is, that they might know the Word of God. And that the eyes of their understanding might be enlightened, that they might know something of the hope of the calling they had in Christ. This is the prayer of the apostle Paul. And if anyone remembers me in prayer, this is exactly what I want them to pray for—that my eyes (my spiritual eyes) might be open. Also I would like to remember you in prayer that way. I believe the most important thing for you and me today is to know the will of God—and the will of God is the Word of God. We cannot know the Word of God unless the Spirit of God is our Teacher. That is what Paul says over in the first epistle to the Corinthians:

Now we have received, not the spirit of the world, but the Spirit who is of God; that we might know the things that are freely given to us of God. Which things also we speak, not in the words which man's wisdom teacheth, but which the Holy Spirit teacheth, comparing spiritual things with spiritual. But the natural man receiveth not the things of the Spirit of God; for they are foolishness unto him, neither can he know them, because they are spiritually discerned. (1 Corinthians 2:12-14 NSRB)

The reason today that so many don't get anything out of the Bible is simply because they are not letting the Spirit of God teach them. The Word of God is different from any other book, you see, because the natural man cannot receive these things. To him they are foolishness. God has given to us the Spirit that we might know the things that are freely given to us of God. He alone is our Teacher; He alone can take the Word of God and make it real and living to us.

God *wants* to communicate with us through His written Word. But it is a supernatural book, and it will not communicate to us on the natural plane for the very simple reason that only the Spirit of God can take the things of Christ and reveal them to us. Notice this very interesting verse of Scripture:

For what man knoweth the things of a man, except the spirit of man which is in him? Even so the things of God knoweth no man, but the Spirit of God. (1 Corinthians 2:11 NSRB)

In a very succinct and understandable manner, this gives the reason the Spirit of God must be our Teacher. You and I understand each other, but we do not understand God. I believe it is perfect nonsense to talk about a generation gap through which we cannot communicate. While it has always been true that it is difficult for an older person and a younger person to see eye to eye, we can communicate with each other because we are all human beings. We understand each other. But, frankly, I don't understand God unless He is revealed to me. I do not know how God feels. I used to wonder how He would feel at a funeral. Well, I find the Lord Jesus there at the funeral of Lazarus and see that He wept. I know how He feels today. I know how He feels about many things because the Spirit of God through the Word of God has revealed them to me.

When I was pastor in Nashville, Tennessee, I got up one bright morning and looked out my window. During the night about five inches of snow had fallen and covered up all the ugliness with a beautiful blanket. I sat upstairs in my study looking out over the scene when I noticed an elder of my church, who lived next door, come out on his porch with two coal scuttles filled with ashes which he was going to empty in the alley. I saw him stop and look over the landscape, and I just smiled because I knew how he felt—just like I felt, looking out on that snow that had fallen during the night. But when he started down the steps, he slipped. Not wanting to spill the ashes, he held them out and hit one of those steps with a real bump. I couldn't help but laugh. I guess if he had broken his neck I still would have laughed. But I noticed that he looked around, and when he was satisfied that nobody had seen him, he got up with great satisfaction and started out again. About half way out on the sidewalk we had a repeat performance; only this time he fell much farther because it was all the way to the sidewalk. And it looked to me like he bounced when he hit. This time he really scanned the landscape. He didn't want anybody to see what he had done. And I knew how he felt. I would have felt the same way. He got up and looked over the landscape, went out and emptied his ashes, and when he got back to the porch, he looked over the landscape again—I don't think this time to admire the scene but to make good and sure that no one had seen him fall. I didn't say a word until Sunday morning. When I came into the church, I went right by where he sat, leaned down and said, "You sure did look funny yesterday carrying out the ashes!" He looked at me in amazement. He said, "Did you see me?" I said, "Yes." "Well," he said, "I didn't think anybody saw me." And I said, "I thought that. I knew exactly how you felt." You see, he had a human spirit and I had a human spirit—we understood each other. But who can understand God? The Spirit of God. And that is the reason the Holy Spirit teaches us, comparing spiritual things with spiritual.

Renan, the French skeptic, made an attack on the Word of God, as you may know; yet he wrote a *Life of Christ*. His book is divided into two sections, one is the historical section, the other is the interpretation of the life of Christ. As far as the first part is concerned, there probably has never been a more brilliant life of Christ written by any man. But his interpretation of it is positively absurd. It could have been done better by a 12-year-old Sunday school boy. What is the explanation of that? Well, the Spirit of God does not teach you history or give you facts that you can dig out for yourself; a very clever mind can dig out those. But the interpretation is altogether different. The Spirit of God has to do the interpreting, and He alone must be the Teacher to lead us and guide us into all truth. We must have the Spirit of God to open our eyes to see.

And we are told to ask His help. In John 16 the Lord Jesus says,

> *I have yet many things to say unto you, but ye cannot bear them now. Nevertheless, when he, the Spirit of truth, is come, he will guide you into all truth; for he shall not speak of himself, but whatever he shall hear, that shall he speak; and he will show you things to come. He shall glorify me; for he shall receive of mine, and shall show it unto you. All things that the Father hath are mine; therefore said I, that he shall take of mine, and shall show it unto you. A little while, and ye shall not see me; and again, a little while, and ye shall see me, because I go to the Father.* (John 16:12-16 NSRB)

So the Lord Jesus is saying that we are to ask. He has many things for us, and He has sent the Holy Spirit to be the Teacher. Again over in chapter 14 He says,

> *But the Comforter, which is the Holy Ghost, whom the Father will send in my name, he shall teach you all things, and bring all things to your remembrance, whatsoever I have said unto you.* (John 14:26)

The Holy Spirit is the Teacher, and He must be the One to lead us and guide us into all truth, friend. If you ever learn anything through my Bible study program, it will not be because this poor preacher is the teacher, it will be because the Spirit of God is opening up the Word of God to you.

This, then, is the first guideline: Begin with prayer and ask the Spirit of God to be your Teacher.

2 READ THE BIBLE

The second guideline may seem oversimplified. Someone asked a great Shakespearean scholar years ago, "How do you study Shakespeare?" His answer was very terse, "Read Shakespeare." And I would say to you: Read the Word of God. Do you want to know what the Bible has to say? Read the Bible. Over and above what any teacher may give you, it is all-important to read for yourself what the Bible has to say.

Dr. G. Campbell Morgan has written some very wonderful and helpful commentaries on the Bible. In fact, he has a series of books that I recommend on all 66 books of the Bible. I know of nothing that is any better than them, and when I started out as a student, they had a great influence on my study of the Word. It is said of him that he would not put pen to paper until he had read a particular book of the Bible through 50 times. So don't be weary in well doing, friend; just read the Word of God. If you don't get it the first time, read it the second time. If you don't get it the second time, read it the third time. Keep on reading it. We are to get the facts of the Word of God.

There is a very interesting incident over in the book of Nehemiah:

> *And all the people gathered themselves together as one man into the street that was before the water gate; and they spoke unto Ezra, the scribe, to bring the book of the law of Moses, which the Lord had commanded to Israel. And Ezra, the priest, brought the law before the congregation both of men and women, and all who could hear with understanding, upon the first day of the seventh month. And he read from it facing the street that was before the water gate from the morning until midday, before the men and the women, and those who could understand; and the ears of all the people were attentive unto the book of the law.* (Nehemiah 8:1-3 NSRB)

This is a very remarkable passage of Scripture. You see, these people had been in Babylonian captivity 70 years; many of them had never heard the Word of God. It did not circulate much in that day. There were not 100 different translations abroad nor new ones coming off the press all the time. Probably there were just one or two copies in existence, and Ezra had one of those copies. He stood and read before the water gate.

> *So they read in the book in the law of God distinctly, and gave the sense, and caused them to understand the reading.* (Nehemiah 8:8 NSRB)

From the way the account is given, I assume that men of the tribe of Levi were stationed in certain areas among the people. After Ezra had read a certain portion, he would stop to give the people who had listened an opportunity to ask questions of the men who were stationed out there to explain the Bible to them.

> . . . And the Levites caused the people to understand the law; and the people stood in their place. (Nehemiah 8:7 NSRB)

Not only did they read the Word, but they caused the people to understand it.

We need to read the Bible.

There are so many distractions today from the study of the Word of God. And the greatest distraction we have is the church. The church is made up of committees and organizations and banquets and entertainments and promotional schemes to the extent that the Word of God is not even dealt with in many churches today. There are churches that have disbanded the preaching service altogether. Instead they have a time in which the people will be able to express themselves and say what they are thinking. I can't imagine anything more puerile or more of a waste of time than that (although it is a fine excuse to get out of preaching for a lazy preacher who will not read or study the Bible). I find that the people who are more ignorant of the Bible than anyone else are church members. They simply do not know the Word of God. And it has been years since it has been taught in the average church. We need to read the Bible. We need to get into the Word of God— not just reading a few favorite verses, but reading the *entire* Word of God. That is the only way we are going to know it, friend. That is God's method.

WHEN YOU READ THE BIBLE THROUGH

> I supposed I knew my Bible,
> Reading piecemeal, hit or miss,
> Now a bit of John or Matthew,
> Now a snatch of Genesis,
> Certain chapters of Isaiah,
> Certain Psalms (the twenty-third),
> Twelfth of Romans, First of Proverbs—
> Yes, I thought I knew the Word!
> But I found that thorough reading
> Was a different thing to do,
> And the way was unfamiliar
> When I read the Bible through.

You who like to play at Bible,
Dip and dabble, here and there,
Just before you kneel, aweary,
And yawn through a hurried prayer;
You who treat the Crown of Writings
As you treat no other book—
Just a paragraph disjointed,
Just a crude impatient look—
Try a worthier procedure,
Try a broad and steady view;
You will kneel in very rapture
When you read the Bible through!

—Amos R. Wells

Then the third guideline is . . .

3 STUDY THE BIBLE

Someone came to Dr. Morgan, years ago, and said, "You speak as though you are inspired!" Dr. Morgan replied, "Inspiration is 95% perspiration." The Bible needs to be studied. We need to realize that the Spirit of God will not teach us something that we could get ourselves by study. I used to teach the Bible in a Bible Institute, and the classes were made up of all kinds of young folk. Among them were a few very pious individuals, and I understood these young people very well after a period of time—I confess I didn't understand them at first. Their pious facade, I found, covered up a tremendous ignorance and vacuum relative to the Word of God. Some of them would not study the night before an exam. They always would give an excuse that they were busy in a prayer meeting or a service somewhere. I had the feeling that some of them believed that they could put their Bibles under their pillows at night and, as they slept, there would come up through the duck feathers the names of the kings of Israel and Judah! Believe me, it won't come up through the duck feathers. We have to knuckle down and study the Word of God. A fellow student in a Bible class when I was in college said, "Doctor, you have assigned us a section that is very dry." The professor, without even missing a step, said to him, "Then dampen it a little with sweat from your brow." The Bible should be studied, and it is very important to see that. There is a certain knowledge that the Spirit of God is not going to give you. I do not think

He is revealing truth to lazy people. After all, you never learn logarithms or geometry or Greek by reading a chapter of it just before you go to sleep at night!

Now you may be shocked when I say that I do not encourage devotional reading of the Bible. Over a period of years I have learned that a great many people who are very faithful in what they call devotional reading are very ignorant of the Bible. I stayed with a family for over a week when I was holding meetings in a place in middle Tennessee. Every morning at the breakfast table we had devotions. Unfortunately, breakfast was always a little late, and Susie and Willie were rushing to get away to school. I am confident that they didn't even know what was read. Dad was wanting to get away to work, and he generally made the Bible reading very brief. Always he'd say, "Well, I'll read this familiar passage this morning because we don't have much time." And, believe me, we didn't. By the time the reading was over, Susie and Willie left the table like they were shot out of a gun, and Dad got out of there almost as quickly as they did, and Mother was left with the dishes—and I wondered if she had really heard what had been read. I determined right there and then that in my home we wouldn't have devotional reading. I have always encouraged members of my family to read the Bible on their own. That is the reading that is profitable.

Someone is going to say, "But I have my devotions at night after the day is over." Now really, don't you have them right before you go to bed? You've got one foot in bed already, one eye is already closed, and you turn to a passage of Scripture to read. Now, friend, you cannot learn mathematics that way. You cannot learn literature that way. You cannot learn the *Bible* that way. You have to *study* the Word of God. You ought to read it when you can give time to it. And if you can't find time, you ought to *make* time. Set apart 30 minutes or an hour. Or if you do things haphazardly like I do, read 30 minutes one day, perhaps only five minutes the next day, and two or three hours the next day, however it fits into your program. I put down no particular rule except that each person should read for himself, and boys and girls should be encouraged to read the Bible for themselves. Some folks feel that they ought to have devotional reading together. And that is fine, if the Lord leads you to do it, but I guarantee you will not be intelligent Bible students after 20 years of doing it like that. You also need to study the Word of God on your own.

It was said of John Wesley that he was a man of one book. What made him a man of one book? Well, he got up and read the Bible at four and five o'clock every morning—read it in five different languages. Believe me, he studied the Word of God. And you and I need to study the Word; we need to get the meaning of the Bible.

This leads me to the fourth guideline:

4 MEDITATE ON THE BIBLE

Meditation is something that God taught His people. The Word of God was to be before the children of Israel all the time—so that they could meditate on it.

> And these words, which I command thee this day, shall be in thine heart: and thou shalt teach them diligently unto thy children, and shalt talk of them when thou sittest in thine house, and when thou walkest by the way, and when thou liest down, and when thou risest up. And thou shalt bind them for a sign upon thine hand, and they shall be as frontlets between thine eyes. And thou shalt write them upon the posts of thy house, and on thy gates. (Deuteronomy 6:6-9)

Now that is an amazing statement coming from the Lord. He told them to write the Word of God upon the doorposts. In other words, wherever they turned, it was just like looking at billboards. You cannot drive up and down our streets and highways without seeing liquor signs and cigarette signs—billboards galore! Now you can understand why people today drink liquor and why they smoke cigarettes—it is before them all the time. The Lord knew human nature. He knew us. And He told His people to get the Word where they would see it. It was on their doorposts, on their gates, and they wore it on their garments. And they were to talk about it when they were walking. They were to talk about the Word when they sat down. They were to talk about it when they went to bed and until they went to sleep. God asked His people to meditate on His Word.

Now what does it really mean to meditate on the Word of God? There is a very interesting statement over in the First Psalm:

> Blessed is the man who walketh not in the counsel of the ungodly, nor standeth in the way of sinners, nor sitteth in the seat of the scornful. But his delight is in the law of the Lord; and in his law doth he meditate day and night. (Psalm 1:1, 2 NSRB)

To meditate is to ruminate, to bring to mind and consider over and over. Ruminating is what a cow is doing when she is chewing her cud. You know how the old cow goes out of a morning, and while the grass is fresh with dew she grazes. Then when the sun comes up and the weather is hot, the old cow lies down under a tree, or stands there in the shade. You see her chewing and you wonder what in the world that cow is chewing. She will chew there for an hour or two. Well, she is meditating, friend. She is bringing the grass she ate of a morning (we are told that a cow has a complex stomach) out of one chamber and is transferring it to another. In the process she is going over it again, chewing it up good. You and I need to learn to do that in our thought processes. We are to get the Word of God, read it, have it out where we can look at it, then think about it, meditate on it.

Many times in preparing a message I'll take a verse of Scripture and spend hours doing nothing but reading it over and over, checking what others have said about it, and just keep reading it. Finally new truth will break out from that particular passage. I remember hearing Dr. Harry Ironside say that he had heard a lecture on the Song of Solomon which left him dissatisfied. He said that he read the Song of Solomon again, got down on his knees and asked God to give him an understanding of it. He did that again and again—in fact, he did it for weeks and months. Finally new light broke from that book. When I teach the Song of Solomon I generally give his interpretation for two reasons: it satisfies my own mind and heart more than does any other interpretation I have heard, and also I know the man who got it had spent a great deal of time in meditation.

There are folk who write to us saying that the wife listens to our Bible study by radio at home, and the husband listens to it at work, and of an evening at the dinner table they discuss the Scripture that was covered. That is meditation; it is going back over it again. Riding along in the car alone is a good place to take a passage of Scripture and really give thought to it.

How many of you, after you have had "devotions," meditate upon that passage during the day? Most people read it and then forget it—never thinking about it again until it is called to their attention. Or, if they read it at night, they jump into bed as quickly as they can, turn out the light, and go to sleep, forgetting all about it. Meditation is almost a lost art in our contemporary society. Frankly, television in many homes absolutely blots out the possibility for meditation. It is changing the spiritual life of many families today. One of the reasons that our churches are becoming colder and more indifferent to the Word of God is simply because there is that lack of meditation upon the Word of God.

Remember (in Acts, chapter 8) the Ethiopian eunuch who was riding along reading Isaiah. He was actually studying Isaiah, because he was in a passage with which he was having trouble—he did not know what it meant. Here is a man who is reading and studying, and the Spirit of God is going to open the Word of God to him. That is the reason the Holy Spirit had Philip there to explain the chapter to the Ethiopian. It opened up a new world to him, and he came to know Christ. The record says that he went on his way rejoicing. What was making him rejoice? He was meditating, friend. He was going back over that 53rd chapter of Isaiah. Have you ever meditated on that Lamb who was brought as a sheep to the slaughter? Who was He? He came down here and identified Himself with us who like sheep have gone astray and have turned every one to our own way. And the Lord has laid on Him the iniquity of us all. How often do you meditate on these things? Well, the Ethiopian did. It always has been a matter of speculation as to what he did after that. Tradition says that he went back to his land and founded the Coptic church of Ethiopia. That could well be; we do not know. However, the interesting thing is that he went on his way rejoicing, which lets us know that he was meditating on the Word of God.

5 READ WHAT OTHERS HAVE WRITTEN ON THE SCRIPTURES

I know that this is a dangerous rule, because many folk depend on what someone else says about it. Also there are many books on the market today that give wrong teaching concerning the Word of God. We need to test everything that is written by the Bible itself.

However, you and I should consult a good commentary. With each outline of the books of the Bible I list recommended books, commentaries that I have read and have found helpful. You will find it very profitable to read what others have said. Actually you are getting all the distilled sweetness and study of the centuries when you read books written by men who have been guided in their study by the Spirit of God. You and I should profit by this. There have been some wonderful, profound works on the books of the Bible.

In addition to commentaries, a concordance is invaluable. I can recommend three: Young's concordance, Strong's concordance, and Cruden's concordance—take your pick. Also you will need a good Bible dictionary. The Davis Bible dictionary is good if you don't get the wrong edition. *Unger's Bible Dictionary* I can recommend without reservation.

Every teacher and preacher of the gospel has a set of books that he studies. He needs them. Someone asks, "Should he present verbatim what somebody else has written?" No, he should never do that, unless he gives credit to the author. But he has a perfect right to use what others have written. I have been told that some of my feeble messages are given by others, and sometimes credit is given and sometimes no mention is made of the author at all. As far as I'm personally concerned, it makes no difference, but it does reveal the character of the individual who will use someone else's material verbatim and not give credit for it. A professor in seminary solved this problem. When someone asked him if he should quote other writers, he said, "You ought to graze on everybody's pasture, but give your own milk." And that means that you are to read what others have written, but you put it in your own thought patterns and express it your way. You have a perfect right to do that. The important thing is that we should take advantage of the study of other men in the Word of God.

6 OBEY THE BIBLE

For the understanding and the study of the Scriptures, *obedience* is essential. Abraham is an example of this. God appeared to him when He called him out of Ur of the Chaldees and again when he was in the Promised Land. But Abraham ran off to Egypt when famine came, and during this time God had no word for him. Not until Abraham was back in the land did God appear to him again. Why? Because of lack of obedience. Until Abraham obeyed what God had already revealed to him, God was not prepared to give to him any new truth. So it is with us. When we obey, God opens up new truth for us.

Even the gospel which is given to save our souls is given for the very definite purpose of obedience. The greatest document that ever has been written on the gospel is the epistle to the Romans. And Paul put around the gospel this matter of obedience. He begins with it:

By whom we have received grace and apostleship, for obedience to the faith among all nations, for his name. (Romans 1:5)

Again, at the end of Romans Paul comes back to this:

But now is made manifest, and by the scriptures of the prophets, according to the commandment of the everlasting God, made known to all nations for the obedience of faith. (Romans 16:26)

"Obedience of faith" is the last thing Paul says in this epistle. What is between? He sets before us what the gospel is, that great doctrinal section; then he concludes with a section on duty—what we're to do. Paul put around the gospel this matter of obedience.

Obedience to the faith. This is where Adam and Eve went wrong. Eve not only listened to Satan, the enemy of God, but she also disobeyed God.

Obedience to God is very important. And we must recognize that God will not continue to reveal truth to us if we become disobedient. We must obey the Bible if we are to profit from its reading.

Also obedience is important because there are folk who measure Christianity by you and by me. Cowan has well said, "The best way to defend the gospel is to live a life worthy of the gospel." That is the way you prove it is the Word of God.

Four clergymen were discussing the merits of various translations of the Bible. One liked the King James Version best because of its simple, beautiful English. Another liked the American Standard Version because it is more literal and comes nearer to the Hebrew and Greek texts. Still another liked a modern translation because of its up-to-date vocabulary. The fourth minister was silent. When asked to express his opinion, he replied, "I like my mother's translation best. She translated it into life, and it was the most convincing translation I have ever seen."

You will recall that Paul wrote to the Corinthian Christians:

Ye are our epistle written in our hearts, known and read of all men: forasmuch as ye are manifestly declared to be the epistle of Christ ministered by us, written not with ink, but with the Spirit of the living God; not in tables of stone, but in fleshy tables of the heart. (2 Corinthians 3:2, 3)

The gospel is written a chapter a day
By deeds that you do and words that you say.
Men read what you say whether faithless or true.
Say, what is the gospel according to you?

—Author unknown

That little jingle is true, by the way.

Oh, how important it is to obey the Bible! I believe that today Christianity is being hurt more by those who are church members than by any other group. That is one of the reasons that we have all of this rebellion on the outside—rebellion against the establishment, which includes the church. A placard carried by one in a protest march had four words on it; "Church, no; Jesus, yes." Candidly, the lives of a great many in the church are turning people away from the church. There was a barrister in England years ago who was asked why he did not become a Christian. This was his answer, "I, too, might have become a Christian if I had not met so many who said they were Christians." How unfortunate that is! We need to examine our own lives in this connection. How important it is to obey the Word of God!

7 PASS IT ON TO OTHERS

Not only read the Bible, not only study the Bible, not only meditate on the Bible, and not only read what others have written about it, but pass it on to others. That is what we all should do. You will reach a saturation point in the study of the Word unless you do share it with others. God for some reason won't let you withdraw yourself from mankind and become some sort of a walking Bible encyclopedia, knowing everything, while the rest of us remain ignorant. I think that is the reason He said:

> *Not forsaking the assembling of ourselves together, as the manner of some is; but exhorting one another: and so much the more, as ye see the day approaching.* (Hebrews 10:25)

God has told us to be witnesses. He said, "Ye shall be witnesses." He did not say that we should be scholars, walking encyclopedias, or memory books. Do not bury God's truth in a notebook. Someone has said that education is a process by which information in the professor's notebook is transferred to the student's notebook, without passing through the mind of either. Well, there is a great deal of Bible truth like that. It is not practiced, not shared. We are called to be witnesses today, therefore we ought to pass it on to others.

I learned this lesson when I was in seminary. I pastored a little church, as did five other fellows, and we found that when we were graduated, we were at least a year ahead of the other members of the class. Why? Because we were smarter than the others? No. Because we were passing it on. God was able to funnel into us a great deal more than He might have otherwise.

My friend, pass it on.

These, then, are the seven basic guidelines to follow as you take in your hands the Word of God:

1 – Begin with prayer	5 – Read what others have written on the Bible
2 – Read the Bible	
3 – Study the Bible	6 – Obey the Bible
4 – Meditate on the Bible	7 – Pass it on to others

HOW TO STUDY YOUR BIBLE

1 – Begin with prayer	1 Corinthians 2:9-14; John 16:12-15; John 14:26
2 – Read the Bible	Nehemiah 8:1-3
3 – Study the Bible	Nehemiah 8:8
4 – Meditate upon the Bible	Deuteronomy 6:6-9; Psalm 1
5 – Pass the Bible on to others	Hebrews 5:12; Romans 12:7

HOW TO STUDY EACH CHAPTER

LOCATE:

1 – The theme	5 – The command to obey
2 – The most important verse	6 – The promise to claim
3 – The most prominent word	7 – The new truth learned
4 – The teaching about Christ	

Open thou mine eyes, that I may behold wondrous things out of thy law. (Psalm 119:18)

A *HANDY* GUIDE FOR MEMORIZING THE BOOKS OF THE BIBLE:

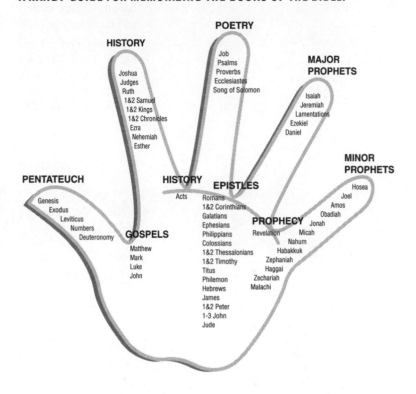

POETRY
Job
Psalms
Proverbs
Ecclesiastes
Song of Solomon

HISTORY
Joshua
Judges
Ruth
1&2 Samuel
1&2 Kings
1&2 Chronicles
Ezra
Nehemiah
Esther

MAJOR PROPHETS
Isaiah
Jeremiah
Lamentations
Ezekiel
Daniel

MINOR PROPHETS
Hosea
Joel
Amos
Obadiah
Jonah
Micah
Nahum
Habakkuk
Zephaniah
Haggai
Zechariah
Malachi

PENTATEUCH
Genesis
Exodus
Leviticus
Numbers
Deuteronomy

HISTORY
Acts

EPISTLES
Romans
1&2 Corinthians
Galatians
Ephesians
Philippians
Colossians
1&2 Thessalonians
1&2 Timothy
Titus
Philemon
Hebrews
James
1&2 Peter
1-3 John
Jude

PROPHECY
Revelation

GOSPELS
Matthew
Mark
Luke
John

Genesis

THE SEED PLOT OF THE BIBLE

The Pentateuch

The first five books of the Bible are called the Pentateuch. Pentateuch means "five books." These books were written by Moses and are identified in Scripture as the Law. Although the Mosaic authorship has been questioned, it is affirmed by conservative scholars and confirmed by archaeology. Bible believers unanimously accept the Mosaic authorship (Deuteronomy 31:9, 24, 26; Acts 7:37, 38).

WRITER: Moses

NAME: The name *Genesis* is taken from the Septuagint. The Septuagint (LXX) is a Greek translation made of the Old Testament in Alexandria at the order of Ptolemy Philadelphus about 285-247 B.C. Josephus tells us that this translation was made by 72 priests (hence its name) in 72 days. Six priests were from each of the 12 tribes. Christ and Paul quoted from this translation of the Old Testament. It is older than any of the Hebrew texts extant today.

Genesis is the book of beginnings and the families—the beginning of creation, man, woman, Sabbath, marriage, family, work, sin, murder, sacrifice, races, languages, culture, civilization, and redemption.

Genesis means "origin," "source," "birth." The meaning closest to that of the original is "birth." It is derived from the Greek verb *gennao*, which means "to beget" or "give birth to." Genesis is the book of beginnings and sources, but more particularly it is the book of births—this is often overlooked. It is the book of generations. According to this understanding of Genesis, it falls into two natural divisions:

- Genesis 2:4—The Book of the Birth of Heaven and the Earth (from Septuagint)
- Genesis 5:1—The Book of the Birth of Men

Simply stated, the book of Genesis is the record of the "family tree" of the Jews. It is the genealogy of heaven, earth, and man. Even the new birth is suggested in Genesis 3:15, where is the first mention of a Redeemer.

OUTLINE (according to genealogies):

Gen. 1:1–2:6	Book of generations of heavens and earth—divine poem of creation—God's creative work
Gen. 2:7–6:8	Book of generations of Adam (men, *anthropoi*)—Adam was created, but children born to him
Gen. 6:9–9:29	Generations of Noah
Gen. 10:1–11:9	Generations of sons of Noah
Gen. 11:10-26	Generations of sons of Shem (Gentiles)
Gen. 11:27–25:11	Generations of Terah
Gen. 25:12-18	Generations of Ishmael
Gen. 25:19–35:29	Generations of Isaac (why Abraham left out, "In Isaac shall thy seed be called" cf. Genesis 21:12; Hebrews 11:8, 9; Romans 9:7)
Gen. 36:1–37:1	Generations of Esau
Gen. 37:2–50:26	Generations of Jacob (genealogy of rejected line given first, chosen line last, cf. 1 Corinthians 15:46 for principle in giving genealogies)

KEY: Generations

PURPOSE: To give us the families—Genesis 12:3; 22:18; 28:13, 14; Acts 3:25; Galatians 3:6, 9, 16.

The first 11 chapters cover a minimum of 2000 years. It could easily be 1000 times longer. From chapter 12 to chapter 50, the time is 350 years. This should arrest our attention.

- 11 chapters cover 2000+ years.
- 39 chapters cover only 350 years.

Certainly the record slows down at chapter 12. Better stated, the first 11 chapters constitute an introduction to the remainder of the book and the Bible. This chart may prove helpful.

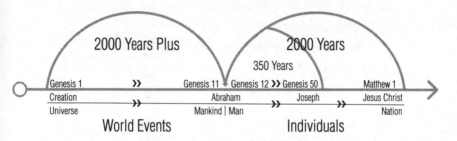

COMMENT: One of the harshest and most frequently heard criticisms of the Bible concerns the creation account. It is pointed out that other nations of antiquity had such a story. This is true, but a comparison of the Genesis record with one of the best of a secular nation, the Babylonian tablets of creation, will show the superiority of the Genesis record. Here all is contrast:

BABYLONIAN	BIBLE
Tablets begin with chaos	Bible begins with cosmos, perfection
Heavenly bodies are gods	Heavenly bodies are matter
Polytheistic theology (many gods)	Monotheistic truth (one God)
Work of a craftsman	God spoke
Characterized by puerility and grotesqueness	Grand and solemn realities of the Creator God who is holy and a Savior
Out of harmony with science	In accord with science (many scientists are believers)

OUTLINE:

I. **Entrance of sin on earth,** Chapters 1–11

A. CREATION, Chapters 1, 2

1. Heaven and Earth, 1:1 *"Create" (bara) occurs only 3 times, vv. 1, 21, 27*

2. Earth became waste and void, 1:2

3. Re-creation, 1:3—2:25

a. First Day—light, 1:3-5

b. Second Day—air spaces (firmament), 1:6-8

c. Third Day—dry land appears and plant life, 1:9-13

d. Fourth Day—sun, moon, stars appear, 1:14-19

e. Fifth Day—animal life (biology), 1:20-23

f. Sixth Day—fertility of creation and creation of man, 1:24-31

g. Seventh Day—Sabbath, 2:1-3

h. Recapitulation of the creation of man, 2:4-25 *(Law of recurrence)*

B. FALL, Chapters 3, 4

1. Root of sin—doubting and disobeying God

2. Fruit of sin— *"Out of the heart proceed ... murders ..."* (Matt. 15:19)

C. FLOOD, Chapters 5–9

1. Book of generations of Adam—through Seth—beginning of man's history—obituary notices, 5

2. Antediluvian civilization—cause of flood and construction of ark, 6

3. Judgment of flood, 7

4. Postdiluvian civilization—after the flood, 8

5. Postdiluvian life—new beginning, 9

D. TOWER OF BABEL and confusion of tongues, Chapters 10, 11

1. Ethnology—sons of Noah, 10

2. Tower of Babel, 11 (Contrast to Day of Pentecost)

II. Preparation for the coming of the Redeemer of all mankind, Chapters 12–50

A. ABRAHAM (faith), Chapters 12–23
(Development of faith by seven appearances of God)

1. God's call and promise to Abram—his response by lapse of faith, 12

2. Abram returns to land from Egypt—separates from Lot—God then appears the third time to Abram, 13

3. First war—Abram delivers Lot; first priest—Abram blessed by Melchizedek, 14

4. God reveals Himself more completely to Abram—reaffirms His promises, 15

5. Unbelief of Sarai and Abram—birth of Ishmael, 16

6. God makes covenant with Abraham (Abram becomes Abraham)—confirms promise to Abraham about a son, 17

7. God reveals coming destruction of Sodom to Abraham—Abraham intercedes on behalf of inhabitants, 18

8. Angels warn Lot—Lot leaves Sodom—God destroys cities of the plain, 19

9. Abraham repeats sin at Gerar about relationship of Sarah, 20

10. Birth of Isaac—Hagar and Ishmael cast out—Abraham at Beer-sheba, 21

11. God commands Abraham to offer Isaac—restrains him—reconfirms covenant with Abraham, 22

12. Death of Sarah—Abraham purchases Machpelah cave for burial place, 23

B. ISAAC (the beloved son), Chapters 24–26
(Choosing of a bride compares with Christ and the church)

1. Abraham sends servant for bride for Isaac—Rebekah returns with him—becomes Isaac's bride, 24

2. Death of Abraham—birth of Esau and Jacob (twins) to Isaac and Rebekah—Esau sells birthright to Jacob, 25

3. God confirms covenant to Isaac—Isaac misrepresents relationship with Rebekah—Isaac digs well in Gerar, 26

C. JACOB ("Whom the Lord loveth He chasteneth"), Chapters 27–36

1. Jacob and Rebekah connive to get blessing intended for Esau, 27

2. Jacob leaves home—at Bethel God appears to him—confirms Abrahamic covenant, 28

3. Jacob arrives in Haran—meets Rachel and Uncle Laban—serves for Rachel—deceived into marrying Leah, 29

4. Birth of sons of Jacob—Jacob prepares to leave Laban—Jacob's bargain pays off, 30

5. Jacob flees from Haran—Laban overtakes him—Jacob and Laban make Mizpah covenant, 31

6. Crisis in life of Jacob: at Peniel a Man wrestles with him—Jacob's name changed to Israel, 32

7. Jacob meets Esau—Jacob journeys to Shalem, 33

8. Scandal in Jacob's family: Dinah defiled—brothers avenge by slaying men of Hamor, 34

9. Jacob returns to Bethel—Rachel dies at Bethlehem—Isaac dies at Hebron, 35

10. Family of Esau which becomes nation of Edom, 36

D. JOSEPH (suffering and glory), Chapters 37–50

1. Jacob dwells in Canaan—Joseph sold into slavery, 37

2. Sin and shame of Judah, 38

3. Humiliation in Egypt, 39, 40

   a. Overseer in house of Potiphar—tempted then framed by wife of Potiphar—imprisoned, 39

   b. Joseph in prison interprets dreams of baker and butler, 40

4. Exaltation in Egypt, 41—48

   a. Joseph interprets dreams of Pharaoh—made overseer of Egypt—marries Asenath—birth of Manasseh and Ephraim, 41

   b. Jacob sends ten sons to Egypt for corn—audience with Joseph—leave Simeon as hostage—return home with corn and refunded money, 42

   c. Jacob sends sons (Benjamin included) again to Egypt—entertained in Joseph's home (does not reveal his identity), 43

d. Joseph sends brothers home—arrested by steward—cup found in Benjamin's sack—Judah pleads for Benjamin, 44

e. Joseph reveals identity—tender reunion with brothers—invites Jacob and all family to Egypt, 45

f. Jacob with family (70) move to Egypt—Jacob and Joseph reunited, 46

g. Jacob and brothers dwell in Goshen—presented to Pharaoh—famine forces Egyptians to sell land to Joseph for Pharaoh—Joseph swears he will bury Jacob in Canaan, 47

h. Jacob on deathbed blesses Joseph's sons, 48

5. Death and burial of Jacob and Joseph, 49, 50

a. Jacob gives deathbed blessing and prophecy for 12 sons, 49

b. Death and burial of Jacob in Canaan—death and burial of Joseph in Egypt, 50

Exodus

Exodus

WRITER: Moses

A CONTINUED STORY: Exodus continues the account that was begun in Genesis, although there was a lapse of at least three and a half centuries. Genesis 15:13 says that the seed of Abraham would spend 400 years in a land that was not theirs. It is difficult to be dogmatic about the chronology of the patriarchal period. It has been omitted purposely from these outlines. The word that opens Exodus is a conjunction, which is better translated "and" rather than "now." Exodus has been called the sequel to Genesis. Dr. G. Campbell Morgan wrote, "In the book of Exodus nothing is commenced, nothing is finished."

MESSAGE: Exodus means "the way out." Redemption is by blood and by power. The message is stated in Hebrews 11:23-29.

KEY VERSE: Exodus 20:2

OUTLINE:

I. A DELIVERER, Chapters 1–11

  A. Slavery of Israel in Egypt, 1

  B. Birth of Moses—first 40 years in Pharaoh's palace, 2

  C. Call of Moses—second 40 years in Midian, 3
     (incident of burning bush)

  D. Return of Moses to Egypt—announcement of deliverance to Israel, 4

  E. Contest with Pharaoh, 5
     (nine plagues against idolatry of Egypt, battle of the gods)

II. DELIVERANCE *(by blood and power),* Chapters 12–14

  A. Institution of Passover—tenth plague, death of firstborn *(blood),* 12

  B. Crossing Red Sea—destruction of army of Egypt *(power),* 13, 14

III. MARCHING to Mt. Sinai *(spiritual education),* Chapters 15–18
     (seven experiences correspond to Christian experience)

  A. Song of redeemed—wilderness of Shur, 15:1-22
     (no bed of roses after redemption)

  B. Marah, bitter water sweetened by tree, 15:23-26
     (Cross sweetens bitter experiences of life)

  C. Elim *(fruitful Christian experience),* 15:27

  D. Wilderness of Sin—manna and quail, 16
     (Christ is the Bread of Life)

  E. Smitten Rock ("That Rock was Christ"), 17:1-7

  F. Amalek *(the flesh),* 17:8-16
     (victory on the hilltop, Deuteronomy 25:17, 18)

  G. Jethro, priest of Midian, 18
     (worldly wisdom in contrast to revelation)

IV. The LAW *(condemnation),* Chapters 19–24

  A. Arrival at Mt. Sinai—agreement to accept the Law, 19

  B. Ten Commandments—order for the altar, 20

  C. Social legislation, 21–24

V. BLUEPRINT and CONSTRUCTION of tabernacle, Chapters 25–40
     (a pattern and picture of Christ)

A. Blueprint for tabernacle—pattern of garments for high priest, 25–30

B. Workmen for tabernacle—Sabbath a sign to Israel, 31

C. Golden calf—broken law—Moses' intercession, second tables of the Law, 32–35

D. Construction of tabernacle, 36–39

E. Tabernacle erected—filled with glory of the Lord, 40

Exodus begins in gloom and ends in glory.

TABERNACLE FLOOR PLAN

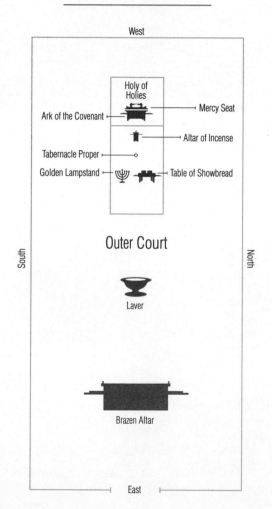

Leviticus

Leviticus

WRITER: Moses

PLACE: In the book of Leviticus the children of Israel were marking time at Mount Sinai. The book opens and concludes at the same geographical spot, Mount Sinai, where God gave the Law. Exodus concludes with the tabernacle constructed and the glory of the Lord filling it. Leviticus gives the order and rules of worship in the tabernacle. The Hebrew word *Vayikrah* opens the book, and it means "and He called." God moves into the tabernacle and speaks from there rather than from Mount Sinai. He calls the people to Him and tells them how to come. This is the exact meaning of the church—*ekklesia*, "called out ones." The Lord Jesus said, "My sheep hear my voice" (John 10:27).

PURPOSE: This is the one book that the critic is categorically convinced should not be in the Bible. Dr. John Haynes Holmes, the humanist, has said, "The book of Leviticus is not fit to be in the Bible." In contradistinction to this extremely biased opinion, others with equal scholarship find it to be a very important book. Dr. S. H. Kellogg called it the "greatest book" in the Bible. Dr. Albert C.

Dudley called it "the most important book in the Bible." Dr. Parker said, "Considered as embracing the history of one month only, this may claim to be the most remarkable book in the Old Testament."

This book was given to Israel for direction in living as a holy nation in fellowship with a holy God. It was a code of law for the total wellbeing of Israel—physical, moral, and spiritual. Sacrifice, ceremony, ritual, liturgy, instructions, washings, convocations, holy days, observances, conditions, and warnings crowd this book. All of these physical exercises were given to teach spiritual truths. Paul states that "these things were our examples" (1 Corinthians 10:6).

Leviticus reveals Christ. Tyndale, in his *Prologue into the Third Book of Moses,* said, "Though sacrifices and ceremonies can be no ground or foundation to build upon—that is, though we can prove nought with them—yet when we have once found Christ and His mysteries, then we may borrow figures, that is to say, allegories, similitudes, and examples, to open Christ, and the secrets of God hid in Christ, even unto the quick: and can declare them more lively and sensibly with them than with all the words of the world."

For us it gives the direction to God and instructions for spiritual worship. Worship would take on a new meaning if the average Christian properly appreciated the contents of this book.

KEY: Holiness to Jehovah

MESSAGE:

The message is twofold:

- Leviticus teaches that **the way to God is by sacrifice**. The word "atonement" occurs 45 times. Atonement means to cover up. The blood of bulls and goats did not actually take away sin. It covered over until Christ came to take away our sins.
- Leviticus teaches that **the walk with God is by sanctification**. The word "holiness" occurs 87 times.

OUTLINE:

I. **The five offerings and the law of them,** Chapters 1–7

A. Sweet savor offerings (person of Christ), 1–3

1. Burnt offering (Christ our substitute), 1

2. Meal offering (loveliness of Christ), 2

3. Peace offering (Christ our peace), 3

Numbers

Numbers

Called Arithmoi *in the Septuagint, meaning "arithmetic"*

WRITER: Moses (see outline of Genesis)

THEME: **"PILGRIM'S PROGRESS"** – walking, wandering, working, warring, witnessing, and worshiping. It is a handbook for pilgrims. "Chart and compass come from Thee." It is a roadmap for the wilderness of this world.

FORWARD MARCH: In the book of Numbers, we see the children of Israel depart from Mt. Sinai and march to Kadesh-barnea. At Kadesh-barnea, the attitude of unbelief is crystallized into actual disobedience. The light is focused on faith, and they failed. "So we see that they could not enter in because of unbelief" (Hebrews 3:19). After Kadesh-barnea, they began to wander until that entire generation died in the wilderness (two notable exceptions were Joshua and Caleb). The years of wandering were a veritable saga of suffering, a trek of tragedy, and a story of straying.

Numbers gets its name from the two censuses recorded in chapters 1 and 26. C. H. Mackintosh called it "a divine history of the wanderings of the Israelites in the wilderness for about 38 years and ten months, commencing with the first movement of the camp after the tabernacle was reared."

KEY PASSAGE: Numbers 14:29-31

These verses outline the experiences of the children of Israel during the time of wandering until the new generation came to the east bank of the Jordan in the land of Moab.

HOW ISRAEL ENCAMPED ON WILDERNESS MARCH
CHART OF CAMP

12 Tribes of Israel

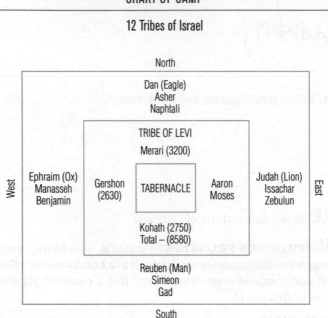

North

Dan (Eagle)
Asher
Naphtali

TRIBE OF LEVI

Merari (3200)

West

Ephraim (Ox)
Manasseh
Benjamin

Gershon
(2630)

TABERNACLE

Aaron
Moses

Judah (Lion)
Issachar
Zebulun

East

Kohath (2750)
Total – (8580)

Reuben (Man)
Simeon
Gad

South

The 40 years of wandering and the unbelief at Kadesh-barnea are not recorded in the "faith" chapter of Hebrews (chapter 11). The record of their unbelief is recorded in Hebrews 3:7-19. This is the "doubting chapter."

THE ORDER BY WHICH THEY MARCHED IS GIVEN IN NUMBERS 10:11-36

SECTION 7	SECTION 6	SECTION 5	SECTION 4	SECTION 3	SECTION 2	SECTION 1
Dan	Ephraim	Kohathites	Reuben	Gershon Merari	Judah "Praise"	Moses Aaron, Ark
bearing standard (v. 25)	*bearing standard* (v. 22)	*bearing sanctuary* (v. 21)	*bearing standard* (v. 18)	*bearing tabernacle* (v. 17)	*bearing standard* (v. 14)	(v. 33)

FORWARD MARCH →

Asher Naphtali	Manasseh Benjamin	Sons of Levi	Simeon Gad	Sons of Levi	Issachar Zebulun	

MIXED MULTITUDE

OUTLINE:

I.   Fitting out the nation Israel for wilderness march, Chapters 1–8
   (Preparation for the pilgrimage)

   A. Order of the camp, Chapters 1–4 *"Let everything be done ... in order."*

   1. First census, Chapter 1

   • *603,550 of those able to go to war (v. 3). Probably 2.5 million came out of Egypt.*

   • *An Israelite must be able to declare his pedigree, know who he is in order to serve and fight.*

   • *A Christian must know his pedigree—"Now are we the sons of God" (1 John 3:2).*

   2. Standards and position of the 12 tribes on wilderness march, Chapter 2
   They had to know where they belonged (see chart) and rally around their standard. Each had his God-appointed place and service.

   3. Census, position, and service of Levites on wilderness march, Chapter 3 *(Census of firstborn)*

   a. Aaron and Moses, vv. 1-4

   b. Tribe of Levi given to Aaron, vv. 5-13 (cf. John 17:6, 9)

   c. Three families of Levi, vv. 14-20

   d. Gershon—in charge of curtains, coverings, and cords, vv. 21-26

   e. Kohath—in charge of articles of furniture, vv. 27-32

   f. Merari—in charge of boards, bars, pillars, sockets, and vessels, vv. 33-37

   g. Total of Levites (22,000), vv. 38, 39

   h. Census of firstborn of all Israel (22,273), vv. 40-51

   4. Service of Levites about the tabernacle, Chapter 4
   (census of Levites [ages 30-50] for service)

   B. Cleansing the camp, Chapters 5–8
   Reason: "Our God is a consuming fire" (Hebrews 12:29)

1. Restitution and jealousy offering, Chapter 5

   a. **Defilement by disease and death,** vv. 1-4
   For the Christian, lepers represent the flesh; the dead represent the world.

   b. **Restitution,** vv. 5-10
   Repentance is more than saying, "I am sorry" (2 Corinthians 7:10).

   c. **Jealousy offering,** vv. 11-31
   "I am a jealous God."

2. Vow of the Nazarite: the triune blessing, Chapter 6

   a. **Nazarite vow,** vv. 1-21
   Voluntary and temporary

      i. **Not to drink wine or strong drink,** v. 3
      His joy is to be in the Lord.

      ii. **Not to shave head,** v. 5
      He is to bear shame (1 Corinthians 11:14).

      iii. **Not to touch dead body,** v. 7
      He is to forsake father and mother.

   b. **Triune blessing,** vv. 22-27

3. Gifts of the princes, Chapter 7
   All give the same. The smallest gift is recorded.

4. Light of lampstand and laver for Levites, Chapter 8

   a. **Light of lampstand,** vv. 1-4
   (Walking in the Light)

   b. **Levites cleansed,** vv. 5-26
   The Christian's cleansing is by the Word.

II. **Forward March!,** Chapters 9, 10

A. Passover and covering cloud, Chapter 9

   1. Passover observed by all on wilderness march, vv. 1-14

   2. Pillar of cloud by day; pillar of fire by night, vv. 15-23

B. Silver trumpets, Chapter 10:1-10
   (Used for moving Israel on wilderness march and calling an assembly)

C. *Forward March!* Order of march, Chapter 10:11-32
   (See chart on page 25.)

D. Halt!, 10:33-36

III. From Sinai to Kadesh, Chapters 11, 12

A. Complaining and murmuring of people displeasing to the Lord, Chapter 11

- Complaining is initiated by the "mixed multitude" (vv. 4-6).
- God provides quail because of dissatisfaction with manna (v. 31).
- When Moses complains, God permits the appointment of elders (v. 16).

B. Jealousy of Miriam and Aaron; judgment of Miriam, Chapter 12
(Rebellion in high places, an infection which delays the march)

IV. Failure at Kadesh, Chapters 13, 14
(Place of decision; great breach of the covenant)

A. Spies chosen and sent into land of Canaan; return and report, Chapter 13

1. Cause for sending spies (cf. Deuteronomy 1:22), vv. 1-3

2. Choice of spies, vv. 4-16

3. Commission of spies, vv. 17-20

4. Conduct of spies, vv. 21-25 *(Did a thorough job)*

5. Confirmation of facts, vv. 26, 27

6. Misinterpretation of facts, vv. 28, 29; 31-33
   (Majority report: giants vs. grasshoppers)

7. Right interpretation of facts, v. 30
   (Minority report: reliance upon God)

B. Israel refuses to enter because of unbelief, Chapter 14
"So we see that they could not enter in because of unbelief" (Hebrews 3:19).

V. Faltering, fumbling and fussing through the wilderness, Chapters 15—25
Silent years—only four incidents recorded—no connected history: (1) log, Numbers 33:19-37; (2) did not circumcise children, Joshua 5:5, 6; (3) did not offer sacrifices to God, Amos 5:25, 26; (4) worshiped idols, Acts 7:42, 43.

A. Delay God's blessing; do not destroy God's purpose, Chapter 15

- *God goes forward; the people go backward. He gives rules for the land. God said they would enter—it was as good as done. 38 years later, Israel, in new generation, enters land. These are the children that the fathers thought might perish (Numbers 14:31).*

- *(Death penalty for breaking Sabbath, vv. 32-36. Do all commandments carry death penalty?)*

B. Incidents relating to the priesthood, Chapters 16 –19

1. Gainsaying of Korah, Chapter 16

   - Fifth murmuring, vv. 1-3
     *Rebellion against divinely constituted authority.
     Korah, a man of great authority, has his place in the
     camp; Moses has his. Rebellion must be dealt with.*

   - Sixth murmuring, v. 41
     Judgment is stayed by Moses.

2. Aaron's rod that budded, Chapter 17

   - Office of Aaron is attested by resurrection (v. 8).

   - Christ is priest after order of Melchizedec, established as
     priest after His resurrection from the dead.

3. Confirmation of priesthood, Chapter 18
   (Charge and position of Aaron and Levites)
   Levites receive tithes and give tithes (v. 26).

4. Offering and ashes of red heifer, Chapter 19
   (Purpose: cleansing the redeemed, cf. Galatians 6:1)

5. Deaths of Miriam and Aaron; water from the rock,
   Chapter 20

   a. At Kadesh again (after 37 years), v. 1

   b. Seventh murmuring, vv. 2-6

   c. Water from rock; disobedience of Moses, vv. 7-13

   d. Edom refuses Israel passage through their land, vv. 14-21

   e. Death of Aaron, vv. 22-29

6. First victory of Israel; first song; serpent of brass,
   Chapter 21

   a. Eighth murmuring, v. 5

   b. Serpent of brass, v. 9 (cf. John 3:14)

   c. Israel sings, v. 17

7. The prophet Balaam, Chapters 22—25

   a. "The way of Balaam"—covetousness, (cf. 2 Peter 2:15, 16), 22

   b. "The error of Balaam"—ignorance of God's righteousness
      (cf. Romans 8:31-34), 23

   c. "The doctrine of Balaam"—fornication with Moabites; embrace their
      idolatry, 24, 25

VI. Future (new) generation prepares to enter land, Chapters 26–36

A. Census of new generation (v. 64), Chapter 26
Less than first census (cf. Numbers 1:46 with Numbers 26:51)

B. Woman's place under law, Chapter 27
Daughters of Zelophehad claim possession of their father. Moses appeals to God for a decision. God grants their request.

C. The law of offerings, Chapters 28, 29
The offerings illustrate the abiding preciousness of Christ, what God thinks of Christ. True worship is thinking God's thoughts after Him.

D. Law of vows, Chapter 30
A vow is inviolate. A woman's vow depends upon her father or husband. The vow of a widow or divorced woman must stand.

E. Judgment of Midian, Chapter 31 (Moses' last act)
Midian in the wilderness is a type of the world. The Christian is to be separated from the world (cf. Galatians 6:14; 1 John 2:15-17).

F. Reuben and Gad ask for land on wrong side of Jordan, Chapter 32
Jordan is a type of death and resurrection of Christ.

G. Log of the journeys, Chapter 33

H. Borders of Promised Land, Chapter 34

I. Cities of refuge given to Levites, Chapter 35
(To be used as refuge for manslayers)

J. Law of land regarding inheritance, Chapter 36
(Land to remain in tribe and family)

Deuteronomy

Deuteronomy

THE BOOK OF EXPERIENCE AND OBEDIENCE

WRITER: Moses. Moses talked with God face to face. Moses knew God. The children of Israel saw the acts of God but did not know Him. Moses knew His ways. Deuteronomy is the result of this intimate knowledge plus the experience of 40 years in the wilderness. Deuteronomy 34:5-12 was probably written by Joshua and belongs to the book of Joshua.

TITLE: Deuteronomy means "second law." This is not to infer that it is a repetition of the Law as given to Moses on Mt. Sinai. It is the Law interpreted in the light of 38 years of experience in the wilderness. New situations and problems arose that were not covered by the Law specifically. There needed to be an application of the Law to life situations.

Deuteronomy, therefore, is more than a mere recapitulation of the Law of Sinai; it is another illustration of the law of recurrence (see 29:1). Specific laws that needed emphasis are repeated and enlarged upon (e.g., the Ten Commandments in chapter 5). Deuteronomy is a commentary on the Mosaic Law.

KEY: Love and obey.

- Love *of* God—4:37; 7:7, 8; 23:5
- Obey God—4:40; 11:26-28; 30:8-20
- Love *for* God—6:4, 5; 30:6, 16, 20

This book teaches man to love and obey God. The word "love" occurs 22 times; "obey" occurs ten times. The motive for obedience is love. The Lord Jesus said, "If ye love me, keep my commandments" (John 14:15). The true motive for obedience is stated in Deuteronomy 6:4, 5. God's love for man is the motive for His government and the giving of laws. Man's love of God is the motive for his obedience. This is not the gospel, but the principle of it is here. This is the pathway of blessing. It is likewise the answer to those who do not find love in the Old Testament. There is love in the Old Testament, and there is law in the New Testament. Moses pleads with them to obey.

WHY OBEY? PLEADING OF MOSES:

1 – Israel belonged to God (14:1)
2 – God loved them (4:37)
3 – God wanted to preserve and prosper them (4:1)
4 – Their show of gratitude (4:7, 8)

COMMENT: A new generation had arrived on the east bank of the Jordan River (1:5) one month before entering the Promised Land (1:3). Those of the generation which had left Egypt were dead and their bones were bleaching beneath the desert skies because of their unbelief and disobedience.

- They had broken God's law—sins of commission;
- They had failed to believe God—sins of omission.

The Law was "weak through the flesh" (Romans 8:3).

Moses gives to this new generation his final instructions from the Lord before he relinquishes leadership of the nation through death.

This new generation was unfamiliar with the experiences of Mt. Sinai, and they needed to have the Law called to their attention and interpreted in the light of their experience and future dwelling in the Promised Land.

The book of Deuteronomy has been the center of attack by the critic. The original criticism was that Moses could not have written it because there was no writing in existence in Moses' day. That has subsequently been soundly refuted. Next the critic stated that the purpose of the book was to glorify the priesthood at Jerusalem, but neither the priesthood nor Jerusalem is mentioned in Deuteronomy.

The probable reason for the satanic attack upon the book of Deuteronomy is that the Lord Jesus Christ quoted exclusively from this book in beating back Satan's temptation. Little wonder Satan hates this book.

First temptation—Matthew 4:4; Luke 4:4	compare Deuteronomy 8:3
Second temptation—Matthew 4:7; Luke 4:12	compare Deuteronomy 6:16
Third temptation—Matthew 4:10; Luke 4:8	compare Deuteronomy 6:13 and 10:20

STRIKING FEATURES:

1 – Greatest doctrinal statement in the Old Testament: Deuteronomy 6:4

2 – First mention of the Great Tribulation: Deuteronomy 4:29-31

3 – Promise of a coming Prophet: Deuteronomy 18:15-18

4 – Test for determining true and false prophets: Deuteronomy 18:20-22

5 – Prewritten history of Israel in the land before they enter the land: Deuteronomy 28–30

6 – Palestinian Covenant: Deuteronomy 29:1–30:10

7 – The Song of Moses—Prophetic: Deuteronomy 32

8 – Lonely and strange death of Moses: Deuteronomy 34:5-8

OUTLINE:

I. Reviewing the journeys, Chapters 1–4

II. Restating the Law—love and obedience, Chapters 5–26

A. Repetition and interpretation of Ten Commandments, Chapters 5–7

B. Religious and national regulations, Chapters 8–21

1. God's past dealings are assurance for future, 8

2. God knew Israel—the past was not good, 9

3. God sent Israel to Egypt; God brought them out of Egypt, 10

4. Promised Land not like Egypt; principle of occupancy, 11

5. Israel has only one place to worship in land, 12

6. Warning against and test of false prophets, false gods, 13

7. Diet for Israel, 14

8. God's poverty program; the permanent slave; the perfect sacrifice is Christ, 15

9. Three main feasts (Passover, Pentecost, Tabernacles); all males required to attend, 16

10. Sundry laws, 17

11. Priests and prophets; test of true prophet, 18

12. Cities of Refuge; extent of land and extremity of Law, 19

13. Laws regulating warfare, 20

14. Laws regulating murder, marriage and delinquent sons, 21

C. Regulations for domestic and personal relations, Chapters 22–26

1. Miscellaneous laws concerning brother relationships, dress, building code, planting seed, and marriage, 22

2. The world, the flesh, and the devil, 23

3. Divorce, 24

4. Punishment of guilty (40 stripes); law protecting widows; punishment for crimes; judgment of Amalek, 25

5. First fruits—thanksgiving, 26

III. Regarding the future of the land, (blessings and curses), Chapters 27–30

IV. Requiem to Moses, Chapters 31–34

One Hebrew division of Deuteronomy is very good and follows the generally accepted pattern:

EIGHT ORATIONS

1st Oration—1:6–4:40	5th Oration—31:1-13
2nd Oration—4:44–26:19	6th Oration—32 (Song of Moses)
3rd Oration—27, 28	7th Oration—33
4th Oration—29, 30	8th Oration—34

Joshua

Joshua

WRITER: Joshua (Joshua 24:26), successor to Moses (Deuteronomy 31:23). The Talmud says that Joshua wrote all but the last five verses and that those were written by Phineas.

"Joshua" means "Jehovah is salvation"—the same word in the New Testament is "Jesus" (as in Hebrews 4:8).

Joshua was a great general, born a slave in Egypt.

40 years old at time of Exodus (one of spies)
80 years old when he received his commission
110 years old at his death

He was a man of prayer, courage, dependence upon God, faith, leadership, enthusiasm, and fidelity. He is a type of Christ in name and work.

PURPOSE: Complete redemption out of Egypt. Salvation is not only a redemption from hell, but it is a redemption to heaven.

TRANSITION: Up to this point Jehovah had spoken by dreams, visions, or by angelic ministry. Now a new method is introduced. The Law of Moses is the written voice of Jehovah (Joshua 1:8).

KEY VERSE: Joshua 1:3

Joshua compares to Ephesians in the New Testament:

> It is prophetic of Israel and typical of the church.
>
> Read Israel's free title to the land (Jeremiah 23:8; Ezekiel 37:21).
>
> Conflict and conquest go with possession.

KEY WORD: Possession.

Israel's *ownership* was unconditional (Genesis 12:7; 15:18-21; 17:8). Israel's *possession* was conditional (Deuteronomy 29:9—30:20). Key word is not "victory"—God gets the victory. Israel gets deliverance and possession.

Joshua 1:4	Extent of Promised Land
Joshua 13:1	They did not possess it all.
Joshua 11:16	Joshua had conquered the land and it was available.
Joshua 11:23	Each tribe was given an allotment but had to drive out the enemy. There was to be a gradual occupation of the land by each tribe.

The Christian today is given title to spiritual blessings (Ephesians 1:3; Romans 5:1-11; Romans 8:37; 1 Corinthians 1:30; Galatians 5:22, 23).

The Christian's practical possession and experience of those blessings depend upon conflict and conquest (Ephesians 6:10-20; Galatians 5:25; 2 Corinthians 10:3-6; 1 Corinthians 9:25-27; Hebrews 4:11). These are never attained through the energy of the flesh, but through the power of the Holy Spirit working in the yielded life of the believer (Romans 7, 8).

OUTLINE:

I. **The land entered,** Chapters 1–12

  A. Commission and command of Joshua, Chapter 1

  B. Contact of spies with Rahab, Chapter 2

  C. Crossing the Jordan River, Chapter 3

  D. Construction of two memorials, Chapter 4

  E. Conditioned for conquest, Chapter 5

  F. Center of land attacked, Chapters 6–8

    1. Conquest of Jericho, 6

    2. Conquest of Ai, 7, 8

  G. Campaign in the south, Chapters 9, 10

    1. Compact with the Gibeonites, 9

    2. Conquer five kings of Amorites (miracle of sun), 10

  H. Campaign in the north, (conclusion of Joshua's leadership in war), Chapter 11

  I. Conquered kings listed, Chapter 12

II. **The land divided,** Chapters 13–22

  A. Command of Joshua is terminated; confirmation of land to the two and a half tribes, Chapter 13

  B. Caleb given Hebron, Chapter 14

  C. Consignment of land to the tribes of Israel, Chapters 15–19

  D. Cities of refuge, Chapter 20

  E. Cities for Levites, Chapter 21

  F. Command to the two and a half tribes to return home; construction of altar as a witness, Chapter 22

III. **The last message of Joshua,** Chapters 23, 24

  A. Call to leaders of Israel for courage and certainty, Chapter 23

  B. Call to all tribes of Israel for consecration and consideration of covenant with God; death of Joshua, Chapter 24

Judges

A PHILOSOPHY OF HISTORY

Righteousness exalteth a nation: but sin is a reproach to any people. (Proverbs 14:34)

WRITER: Unknown. This book comes from the period of the monarchy, judging by the phrase which occurs four times, "In those days there was no king in Israel" (17:6; 18:1; 19:1; 21:25). Probably written by Samuel.

KEY VERSE: Judges 21:25 (last verse in the book)

THEME: Backsliding—and the amazing grace of God in recovering and restoring.

PURPOSE: The book of Judges serves a twofold purpose:

1 Historically it records the history of the nation from the death of Joshua to Samuel, the last of the judges and the first of the prophets. It bridges the gap between Joshua and the rise of the monarchy. There was no leader to take Joshua's place in the way he had taken Moses' place. This was the trial period of the theocracy after they entered the land.

2 Morally it is the time of the deep declension of the people as they turned from the Unseen Leader and descended to the low level of "In those days there was no king in Israel, but every man did that which was right in his own eyes"

(Judges 17:6; also compare Judges 1:1 with 20:18). This should have been an era of glowing progress, but it was a dark day of repeated failure.

This course can be plotted like a hoop rolling down the hill of time. The steps of a nation's downfall are outlined in the last division of the book (see outline). Isaiah, chapter 1, presents these same fatal steps downward that eventually led to the final captivity of the nation.

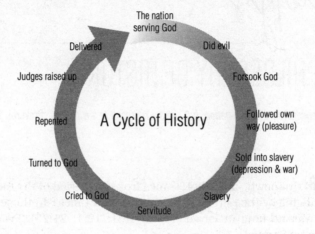

A Cycle of History

The nation serving God

Did evil

Forsook God

Followed own way (pleasure)

Sold into slavery (depression & war)

Slavery

Servitude

Cried to God

Turned to God

Repented

Judges raised up

Delivered

OUTLINE:

I.   Introduction to era of the judges, Chapters 1, 2

A. Condition of nation after death of Joshua (revealed in limited victories of tribes of Judah, Simeon, Benjamin, Manasseh, Ephraim, Zebulun, Asher, Naphtali, Dan), Chapter 1

B. God feeds into computer of history Israel's cycle in period of the judges, Chapter 2

II.   Era of the judges, Chapters 3–16

A. First Apostasy; conquered by Mesopotamia; delivered through Othniel, the judge, Chapter 3:1-11

B. Second Apostasy; conquered by Moabites and Philistines; delivered through Ehud and Shamgar, the judges, Chapter 3:12-31

C. Third Apostasy; conquered by Jabin, king of Canaan; delivered through Deborah and Barak, the judges, Chapters 4:1–5:31

D. Fourth Apostasy; conquered by Midian; delivered through Gideon, the judge, Chapters 6:1–8:32

E. Fifth Apostasy; civil war; delivered through Abimelech, Tola, Jair, the judges, Chapters 8:33–10:5

F. Sixth Apostasy; conquered by Philistines and Ammonites; delivered through Jephthah, Ibzan, Elon, Abdon, the judges, Chapters 10:6–12:15

G. Seventh Apostasy; conquered by Philistines; delivered partially through Samson, the judge, Chapters 13–16

III.   Results of era of the judges (confusion), Chapters 17–21

A. Religious apostasy (the temple), Chapters 17, 18

B. Moral awfulness (the home), Chapter 19

C. Political anarchy (the state), Chapters 20, 21

Ruth

_An addendum to the book of Judges. A brochure of beauty.
A bright picture on the black background of the judges._

WRITER: Samuel could have been the writer.

KEY VERSE: Ruth 3:18

THEME: The kinsman-redeemer

FEATURES:

1 – A love story without using the word "love."

2 – The story of a prodigal family who went to the far country.

3 – The only example of the law of the kinsman-redeemer (Hebrew _goel_) in action. Also shows how other laws of the Mosaic system operated.

4 – Furnishes the link between the tribe of Judah and David. The genealogy at the end of the book becomes a most important document. It is found again in the first chapter of Matthew.

5 – A lovely picture of Christ and the church.

COMMENT: To appreciate this love story in all of its tenderness, sweetness, and loveliness, read or listen to it in the complete 5-year _Thru the Bible_ series. Find all of your options at www.TTB.org/Ruth.

OUTLINE:

1 & 2 Samuel

1 & 2 Samuel

I gave thee a king in mine anger, and took him away in my wrath. (Hosea 13:11)

The books of 1 and 2 Samuel give us the origin of the kingdom. The two books of Samuel were classified as one in the Jewish canon. They are the first two of four books of Kings in the Latin Vulgate.

WRITER: The name of Samuel is identified with these two historical books, not because he was the writer primarily, but because his story occurs first and is so prominent. He anointed as king both Saul and David. Samuel is considered the author up to 1 Samuel 25 (his death). Nathan and Gad completed the writing (1 Chronicles 29:29 ASV).

FEATURES:

1 – The rise of the kingdom.	6 – King Saul's visit to witch of Endor.
2 – The story of Hannah.	7 – God's covenant with David in 2 Samuel 7.
3 – The story of little Samuel.	8 – David's great sin—Bathsheba.
4 – The story of David and Goliath.	9 – David's rebellious son—Absalom.
5 – The friendship of David and Jonathan.	

THEME:

Prayer	1 Samuel opens with prayer; 2 Samuel closes with prayer.
Kingdom	The change of the government from a theocracy to a kingdom; God's covenant with David.
Prophet	The rise of the office of prophet, who became the messenger of God in place of the priest.

KEY VERSE: 1 Samuel 10:25

COMMENT: There is a striking contrast between the characters in the book of Judges and those in the two books of Samuel. The men in Judges seem to be ordinary and average, while here the characters are outstanding and above the average. There are six who stand out in 1 Samuel. They are Hannah, Eli, Samuel, Saul, Jonathan, and David. First Samuel is a transitional book from the era of the judges to the kingdom. The kingdom foreshadows the coming millennial kingdom in some respects. There are certain profound global lessons for us in the setting up of the kingdom. The world needs:

1 – A king with power who exercises his power righteously
2 – A king who will be in full dependence upon God and who can be trusted with power
3 – A king who is in full obedience to God

CHAPTERS AND VERSES WORTH REMEMBERING:

1 Samuel 15:22	Samuel's word about obedience
1 Samuel 25:29	Abigail's word about David's relationship to God
2 Samuel 3:33	Abner's epitaph
2 Samuel 7	God's covenant with David (note the seven "I wills")
2 Samuel 18:33	David's grief over Absalom
2 Samuel 22	Song of David (Psalm 18)
2 Samuel 24:24	David's rebuke against a cheap religion

1 SAMUEL

OUTLINE:

I. **SAMUEL: God's prophet, priest, and judge,** Chapters 1–8

A. Birth of Samuel, Chapters 1, 2

   1. Hannah's prayer and answer, 1

   2. Hannah's prophetic prayer; boy Samuel in temple, 2

B. Call of Samuel, Chapter 3

C. Last judge and first prophet (prophetic office), Chapters 4–8

   1. Ark captured by Philistines; Word of God to Samuel fulfilled; Eli dies and his sons slain, 4

   2. God judged Philistines because of the ark; ark returned to Bethshemesh, 5, 6

   3. Samuel leads in revival (put away idols and turn to Jehovah); victory at Ebenezer, 7

   4. Israel rejects God and demands a king; Samuel warns nation but promises a king, 8

II. **SAUL: Satan's man,** Chapters 9–15

A. Saul received, Chapters 9, 10

   1. Saul chosen as king, 9

   2. Saul anointed as king, 10

B. Saul reigning, Chapters 11, 12

   1. Saul's victory over Ammonites, 11

   2. Transfer of authority from Samuel to Saul, 12

C. Saul rejected, Chapters 13–15

   1. Saul's rebellion against God, 13

   2. Jonathan responsible for victory over Philistines; Saul took credit, 14

   3. Saul's glaring rebellion and disobedience regarding Agag, 15

III. **DAVID: God's man, and SAUL: Satan's man,** Chapters 16–31

A. David anointed, Chapter 16

B. David trained, Chapters 17, 18

1. David slays Goliath, giant of Gath, 17

2. Jonathan and David make covenant; Saul gives daughter Michal to David, 18

C. David disciplined, Chapters 19–30

1. Saul attempts to kill David again, 19

2. Jonathan helps David escape, 20

3. David escapes to Nob and Gath, 21

4. David gathers his men; Saul slays priests of God, 22

5. David fights Philistines; Saul pursues David; Jonathan and David make covenant, 23

6. David spares Saul's life at En-gedi, 24

7. Samuel dies; David and Abigail, 25

8. David again spares Saul's life in wilderness of Ziph, 26

9. David retreats to land of Philistia (Ziklag), 27

10. Saul goes to witch of Endor, 28

11. Philistines do not trust David in battle, 29

12. David fights Amalekites because of destruction of Ziklag, 30

D. Saul, mortally wounded in battle, commits suicide, Chapter 31

2 SAMUEL

COMMENT: The book of 2 Samuel continues the message of 1 Samuel. It is given over entirely to the reign of David. The life and times of David are important because he is the ancestor of Jesus (Matthew 1:1). It shows that government of this world in the hands of man is a failure.

OUTLINE:

I. **TRIUMPHS of David,** Chapters 1–10

   A. David mourns the deaths of Saul and Jonathan, Chapter 1

   B. David made king over Judah, Chapter 2

   C. Civil war—Abner joins with David but murdered by Joab, Chapter 3

   D. Ish-bosheth, son of Saul, killed, Chapter 4

   E. David made king over all Israel; moves his capital to Jerusalem, Chapter 5

   F. David's wrong and right attempts to bring the ark to Jerusalem, Chapter 6

   G. God's covenant to build the house of David, Chapter 7

   H. David consolidates his kingdom, Chapter 8

   I. David befriends Mephibosheth, Chapter 9

   J. David wars against Ammon and Syria, Chapter 10

II. **TROUBLES of David,** Chapters 11–24

   A. David's two great sins, Chapter 11

   B. Nathan faces David with his sins; David repents, Chapter 12

   C. David's daughter Tamar raped by Amnon, David's son; Amnon murdered by Absalom, David's son, Chapter 13

   D. David permits Absalom to return with half-hearted forgiveness, Chapter 14

   E. Absalom rebels against David, Chapter 15

   F. Ziba, Mephibosheth's servant, deceives David; Shimei curses David, Chapter 16

   G. Absalom's advisers (Ahithophel and Hushai) disagree on attack against David, Chapter 17

   H. Absalom slain and David mourns, Chapter 18

   I. David restored to throne, Chapter 19

1 & 2 Kings

1 & 2 Kings

The second in the series of three double books. Originally one book, they were divided by the Septuagint translators.

WRITER: Although the writer is unknown, it was written while the first temple was still standing (1 Kings 8:8). Jeremiah is the traditional writer. Modern scholarship assigns the authorship to "the prophets."

THEME: Standard of the kingdom: "as David his father" (repeated nine times in 1 Kings). It was a human standard, but man failed to attain even to it.

KEY VERSES: 2 Kings 17:22, 23 and 25:21

FEATURES:

1 - Practically all the rulers were evil.

2 - God's patience in dealing with them.

3 - Names of the mothers are given of both good and bad kings.

4 - God's grace in sending revival when the king, with the people, turned to Him.

5 - Prominence of the prophet and insignificance of the priest.

> 6 – God's long delay before the captivity of both Israel and Judah.
>
> 7 – Man's total inability to rule for God.
>
> 8 – Wicked kings who had godly sons, also good kings who had wicked sons.

KINGDOM: First Kings records the *division* of the kingdom; Second Kings records the *collapse* of the kingdom. Considered together, they open with King David and close with the king of Babylon. They are the book of man's rule of God's kingdom. The throne on earth must be in tune with the throne in heaven if blessings come and benefits accrue to the people. Yet man's plan cannot overthrow God's purposes.

PURPOSE: It is a continuation of the narrative begun in 1 & 2 Samuel. Actually, 1 & 2 Samuel with 1 & 2 Kings can be viewed as one book. In these four books the history of the nation is traced from the time of its greatest extent, influence, and prosperity under David and Solomon to the division and finally the captivity and exile of both kingdoms.

The moral teaching is to show man his inability to rule himself and the world. In these four historical books we have the rise and fall of the kingdom of Israel.

OUTLINE:

I. **Death of David,** 1 Kings 1, 2

II. **Glory of Solomon's reign,** 1 Kings 3–11

  A. Solomon's prayer for wisdom, Chapters 3, 4

  B. Building of the Temple, Chapters 5–8

  C. Fame of Solomon, Chapters 9, 10

  D. Shame and death of Solomon, Chapter 11

III. **Division of the kingdom,** 1 Kings 12–2 Kings 16
    (See table on next pages)

IV. **Captivity of Israel by Assyria,** 2 Kings 17

V. **Decline and captivity of Judah by Babylon,** 2 Kings 18–25

CHRONOLOGICAL TABLE OF THE KINGS OF THE DIVIDED KINGDOM

JUDAH

KING	REIGN	CHARACTER	PROPHET
1 – Rehoboam	931-913 B.C. (17 years)	Bad	Shemaiah
2 – Abijah	913-911 B.C. (3 years)	Bad	
3 – Asa	911-870 B.C. (41 years)	Good	
4 – Jehoshaphat	870-848* B.C. (25 years)	Good	
5 – Jehoram	848-841* B.C. (8 years)	Bad	
6 – Ahaziah	841 B.C. (1 year)	Bad	
7 – Athaliah	841-835 B.C. (6 years)	Bad	
8 – Joash	835-796 B.C. (40 years)	Good	Joel
9 – Amaziah	796-767 B.C. (29 years)	Good	
10 – Azariah (or Uzziah)	767-740* B.C. (52 years)	Good	Isaiah
11 – Jotham	740-732* B.C. (16 years)	Good	Micah
12 – Ahaz	732-716 B.C. (16 years)	Bad	
13 – Hezekiah	716-687 B.C. (29 years)	Good	
14 – Manasseh	687-642* B.C. (55 years)	Bad	
15 – Amon	642-640 B.C. (2 years)	Bad	Nahum
16 – Josiah	640-608 B.C. (31 years)	Good	Habakkuk
17 – Jehoahaz	608 B.C. (3 months)	Bad	Zephaniah
18 – Jehoiakim	608-597 B.C. (11 years)	Bad	Jeremiah
19 – Jehoiachin	597 B.C. (3 months)	Bad	
20 – Zedekiah	597-586 B.C. (11 years)	Bad	

DESTRUCTION OF JERUSALEM AND CAPTIVITY OF JUDAH
*Co-regency

CHRONOLOGICAL TABLE OF THE KINGS OF THE DIVIDED KINGDOM

ISRAEL

KING	REIGN	CHARACTER	PROPHET
1 – Jeroboam I	931-910 B.C. (22 years)	Bad	Ahijah
2 – Nadab	910-909 B.C. (2 years)	Bad	
3 – Baasha	909-886 B.C. (24 years)	Bad	
4 – Elah	886-885 B.C. (2 years)	Bad	
5 – Zimri	885 B.C. (7 days)	Bad	
6 – Omri	885-874* B.C. (12 years)	Bad	Elijah
7 – Ahab	874-853 B.C. (22 years)	Bad	Micaiah
8 – Ahaziah	853-852 B.C. (2 years)	Bad	
9 – Joram	852-841 B.C. (12 years)	Bad	Elisha
10 – Jehu	841-814 B.C. (28 years)	Bad	
11 – Jehoahaz	814-798 B.C. (17 years)	Bad	Jonah
12 – Jehoash	798-782 B.C. (16 years)	Bad	Amos
13 – Jeroboam II	782-753* B.C. (41 years)	Bad	Hosea
14 – Zechariah	753-752 B.C. (6 months)	Bad	
15 – Shallum	752 B.C. (1 month)	Bad	
16 – Menahem	752-742 B.C. (10 years)	Bad	
17 – Pekahiah	742-740 B.C. (2 years)	Bad	
18 – Pekah	740-732* B.C. (20 years)	Bad	
19 – Hoshea	732-721 B.C. (9 years)	Bad	

CAPTURE OF SAMARIA AND CAPTIVITY OF ISRAEL
*Co-regency

1 & 2 Chronicles

1 & 2 Chronicles

THE ACTS OF THE OLD TESTAMENT

WRITER: Probably Ezra. There is a striking resemblance in style and language to the books of Ezra and Nehemiah. Evidently Chronicles was written during the Babylonian captivity. It could have been a compilation, assembled by Ezra, of diaries and journals of the priests and prophets. These two books of Chronicles not only constituted one book in the original, but apparently also included Ezra and Nehemiah. This lends support to the authorship of Ezra and supports the Jewish tradition. Scholars have noted a similarity in the Hebrew of all four books.

COMMENT: Many treat Chronicles and Kings as if they were "Cabbages and Kings." Are the Chronicles a duplication of Kings? Although they cover the same ground from Saul to Zedekiah, they are not duplications. Greek translators gave Chronicles the title of "Things Omitted"—there is more here that does not occur in the other historical books. This is another instance of the law of recurrence or recapitulation, seen previously in Genesis 2 and Deuteronomy, by which God goes over previously covered ground in order to add details and emphasize that which He considers important. This is exactly the case in Chronicles. David is the subject of 1 Chronicles; the house of David is prominent in 2 Chronicles.

Chronicles gives the history of Judah while practically ignoring the northern kingdom. Chronicles does not record David's sin—when God forgives, He forgets. The temple and Jerusalem are prominent in Chronicles. In Kings, the history of the nation is given from the throne; in Chronicles, it is given from the altar. The palace is the center in Kings; the temple is the center in Chronicles. Kings records the political history; Chronicles records the religious history. Chronicles is an interpretation of Kings—hence the constant reference in Kings to Chronicles. Kings gives us man's viewpoint; Chronicles gives us God's viewpoint (note this well as you read Chronicles; it will surprise you).

1 CHRONICLES

OUTLINE:

I.   Genealogies, Chapters 1–9
This is important to God. We must be sons of God before we can do the work of God. "Ye must be born again" (John 3:7). These help explain the two genealogies of Christ in Matthew and Luke (compare 1 Chronicles 3:5 with Luke 3:31).

II. Saul's reign, Chapter 10

III. David's reign, Chapters 11–29

A. David's mighty men, Chapters 11, 12

B. David and the ark, Chapters 13–16

C. David and the temple, Chapter 17

D. David's wars, Chapters 18–20

E. David's sin in numbering the people, Chapter 21

F. David's preparation and organization for building the temple, Chapters 22–29

2 CHRONICLES

OUTLINE:

I. **Solomon's reign,** Chapters 1–9
   Building the temple is his most important accomplishment.

II. **Division of the kingdom and the history of Judah,** Chapters 10–36
   Reformations given prominence:

A. **Asa's,** Chapters 14–16

B. **Jehoshaphat's,** Chapters 17–20

C. **Joash's,** Chapters 23, 24

D. **Hezekiah's,** Chapters 29–32

E. **Josiah's,** Chapters 34, 35

Ezra

Ezra

Post-Captivity Books

The post-captivity books record the return and restoration at Jerusalem after the 70-year Babylonian captivity as predicted by Jeremiah. Six books belong to this series. They are divided into two groups:

- Historical—Ezra, Nehemiah and Esther;
- Prophetical—Haggai, Zechariah and Malachi.

Although Ezra is a continuation of the historical books begun with Joshua, the pre-captivity and captivity books could be profitably studied before beginning with Ezra. These books include all of the major and minor prophets, with the exception of the last three books of the Old Testament. However, we shall proceed according to the arrangement of the canon of Scripture.

WRITER: Ezra. He is one character who has not received proper recognition. He was a descendant of Hilkiah (Ezra 7:1), the high priest who found a copy of the Law during the reign of Josiah (2 Chronicles 34:14). Ezra, as a priest, was unable to serve during the captivity, but he gave his time to a study of the Word of God—he was "a ready scribe in the law of Moses" (Ezra 7:6). Ezra was a great revivalist and reformer. The revival began with the reading of the

Word of God by Ezra (Nehemiah 8). Also, he probably was the writer of 1 and 2 Chronicles and of Psalm 119, which exalts the Word of God. He organized the synagogue, founded the order of scribes, helped settle the canon of Scripture and arranged the Psalms.

Let us pay tribute to Ezra who was the first to begin a revival of Bible study. Is this not God's program for revival?

THEME: The Word of the Lord. (There are 11 direct references—1:1; 3:2; 6:14, 18; 7:6, 10, 14, 26; 9:4; 10:3, 5.)

The place of the Word of God in the total life of His people—religious, social, business, and political.

KEY PHRASE: "Trembled at the words of the God of Israel" (Ezra 9:4; also see 10:3).

OUTLINE:

I. **RETURN from BABYLON LED by ZERUBBABEL,** Chapters 1–6
    (About 50,000 returned)

   A. Restoration of temple by decree of Cyrus, Chapter 1

   B. Return under Zerubbabel, Chapter 2

   C. Rebuilding of temple, Chapter 3

   D. Retardation of rebuilding of temple by opposition, Chapter 4
      (Decree of Artaxerxes)

   E. Renewal of rebuilding of temple, Chapters 5, 6
      (Decree of Darius)

II. **RETURN from BABYLON LED by EZRA,** Chapters 7–10
    (About 2,000 returned)

   A. Return under Ezra, Chapters 7, 8

   B. Reformation under Ezra, Chapters 9, 10

      1. Prayer of Ezra, Chapter 9

      2. Separation from heathen is demanded and maintained, Chapter 10

The books of Haggai and Zechariah (Ezra 5:1) should be read and studied with the book of Ezra, for all three were written in the shadow of the rebuilt temple and were given to encourage the people in building.

Nehemiah

Nehemiah

(Ezra and Nehemiah are one book in the Hebrew canon.)

WRITER: Perhaps Ezra. Nehemiah was a layman; Ezra was a priest. In the book of Ezra, the emphasis is upon the rebuilding of the temple; in the book of Nehemiah, the emphasis is upon the rebuilding of the walls of Jerusalem. In Ezra, we have the religious aspect of the return; in Nehemiah, we have the political aspect of the return. Ezra is a fine representative of the priest and scribe; Nehemiah is a noble representative of the businessman. Nehemiah had an important office at the court of the powerful Persian king, Artaxerxes, but his heart was with God's people and God's program in Jerusalem. The personal note is the main characteristic of the book.

DATE: Chronologically, this is the last of the historical books. We have come to the end of the line as far as time is concerned. The Old Testament goes no further. The book of Ezra picks up the thread of the story about 70 years after 2 Chronicles. The 70-year captivity is over and a remnant returns to the land of Israel. The return under Ezra takes place about 50 years after Zerubbabel. Nehemiah returns about 15 years after Ezra. These figures are approximate and are given to show the stages in the history of Israel after the captivity. This enables one to see how the "70 weeks" of

Daniel fit into the picture in a normal and reasonable way. The "70 weeks" of Daniel begin with the book of Nehemiah (not with Ezra) "from the going forth of the commandment to restore and to build Jerusalem unto the Messiah, the Prince, shall be seven weeks, and threescore and two weeks ...." The background of the events of Nehemiah is "... the street shall be built again, and the wall, even in troublous times" (Daniel 9:25).

Note: The following dates, suggested by Sir Robert Anderson, seem to be a satisfactory solution to the problem of the "70 weeks" of Daniel:

Decree of Cyrus, 536 B.C.—Ezra 1:1-4
Decree of Artaxerxes, 445 B.C. (twentieth year of his reign)—Nehemiah 2:1-8
The "70 weeks" begin. The first "seven weeks" end, 397 B.C.—Malachi.

(For details see Sir Robert Anderson's *The Coming Prince*)

KEY WORD: "So" occurs 32 times. It denotes a man of action and few words. Mark this word in your Bible and notice how this ordinarily unimportant word stands out in this book.

KEY VERSES: Nehemiah 1:4 and 6:3

OUTLINE:

I. **REBUILDING the WALLS,** Chapters 1–7

A. Nehemiah's prayer for remnant at Jerusalem, Chapter 1

B. Nehemiah's request of the king, return to Jerusalem, and review of ruins of Jerusalem, Chapter 2:1-16

C. Nehemiah's encouragement to rebuild the walls, Chapter 2:17-20

D. Rebuilding the walls and gates, Chapter 3

E. Nehemiah's response to opposition, Chapters 4–6
Wall completed, 6:15

F. Nehemiah's register of people, Chapter 7
(Only 42,360 people, 7,337 servants, and 245 singers returned. Compare this with the fact that Judah alone had 470,000 warriors [1 Chronicles 21:5].)

II. **REVIVAL and REFORM,** Chapters 8–13

A. Great Bible reading led by Ezra, Chapter 8

B. Revival—the result, Chapters 9, 10

C. Reform—another result, Chapters 11–13

THE BABYLONIAN CAPTIVITY: God's chosen people were called to witness against idolatry, but too often they themselves succumbed and became idolaters. God sent them to Babylon, the fountainhead of idolatry, to take the gold cure. They returned repudiating idolatry.

Their restoration as an independent nation was incomplete. They were not free from this time on to the time of the Roman Empire. The New Testament opens with them under the rule of Rome.

Eighter

Esther

This is one of the two books of the Old Testament named for a woman. While Ruth is the story of a Gentile who married a Jew, Esther is the story of a Jewess who married a Gentile.

WRITER: Unknown. Could Mordecai have been the writer? (See Esther 9:29.)

KEY VERSE: Esther 4:14

A STRANGE STORY: God's name is not mentioned in this book; no divine title or pronoun refers to Him. The heathen king's name is mentioned 192 times. (It is true also that God's name does not occur in the Song of Solomon, but every masculine pronoun—with a possible exception of 8:6—refers to Him.) Esther is the record of Israel in a self-chosen pathway. Opportunity had been given for the Jews to return under Cyrus, but only a very small remnant returned. Ezra and Nehemiah give the story of those who did return; Esther gives the story of those who did not return but who chose instead the prosperity and luxury of Persia. They are out of the will of God, but they are not beyond His care. Deuteronomy 31:18 explains the reason God's name does not appear. In the book of Esther His face is hidden. There is no mention of prayer nor dependence upon God in this book. Esther is never quoted in the New Testament, nor is there even a casual reference to it.

However, the Jews give it a peculiar emphasis. It is one of the five books called *Megilloth* (rolls) and is placed beside the Pentateuch in importance.

SUBJECT: Esther teaches the providence of God. "Providence" comes from the same stem as "provide," and it means simply that God will provide.

Theologically, providence is the direction God gives to everything: animate and inanimate, good and evil.

Practically, providence is the hand of God in the glove of history—and that glove will never move until He moves it. God is at the steering wheel of this universe. Providence means that God is behind the scenes, shifting and directing them. Providence is the way God coaches the runner on second base. It is the way God leads those who will not be led. As recorded in the book of Esther, the entire Jewish nation would have been slain had it not been for the providence of God. God stands in the shadows, keeping watch over His own.

ANTI-SEMITISM: This book teaches how God met another satanic attempt to destroy the nation Israel, and how vengeance was wrought upon the perpetrators of the dastardly deed. (See Genesis 12:3.)

OUTLINE:

Poetical Books

Job is the first of the poetical books, which also include Psalms, Proverbs, Ecclesiastes, Song of Solomon, and Lamentations. The reference is to the *form* of the content and does not imply imaginative or capricious content. Neither does the term "poetical" mean that it is rhythmic. Hebrew poetry is achieved by repeating an idea, a technique called parallelism. The dialogue in the book of Job is poetry because conversation was in poetry in that day. The *Iliad* and *Odyssey* of Homer are examples in secular literature.

WRITER: Unknown. The following have been suggested: Moses, Ezra, Solomon, Job and Elihu. That Elihu is the writer seems most likely (32:16).

DATE: Unknown. Evidently it was written during the patriarchal period. Did Job know Jacob? It is possible. It was written before Exodus, it would seem, as there is no reference to the Mosaic Law nor to any of the events recorded in the book of Exodus. Here are the arguments which seem to place Job with the patriarchs:

1 – Length of Job's life span (42:16).

2 – Job acted as high priest in his family.

3 – Eliphaz the Temanite was descended from Esau's eldest son (Genesis 36:10, 11).

103

PURPOSE: Many problems are raised and settled in this book.

1 – To determine why the righteous suffer. (This is not the primary teaching.)
2 – To refute the slander of Satan.
3 – To reveal Job to himself.
4 – To teach patience. Was Job patient?
5 – *Primary purpose*: To teach *repentance*.

God selected the best man who ever lived (Christ is the exception) and showed that he needed to repent. In contrast, we usually choose the worst man who repents as an illustration. Manasseh, a most ungodly king, repented; Saul of Tarsus repented; St. Francis of Assisi, a debauched nobleman, repented; and Jerry MacAuley, a drunken bum, repented. God chose the best man and showed that he repented—"I have heard of thee by the hearing of the ear: but now mine eye seeth thee. Wherefore I abhor myself, and repent in dust and ashes" (Job 42:5, 6).

ESTIMATION: Tennyson said of the book of Job, "The greatest poem, whether of ancient or modern literature." Carlyle said, "I call [Job] one of the grandest ever written with pen." Luther said, "More magnificent and sublime than any other book of Scripture." Moorehead said, "The book of Job is one of the noblest poems in existence."

OUTLINE:

I.   DRAMA, Chapters 1, 2
(Prose)

A. **Scene I,** Chapter 1:1-5
Land of Uz; Job's prosperity and serenity

B. **Scene II,** Chapter 1:6-12
Heaven; Satan's slander of God and Job

C. **Scene III,** Chapter 1:13-22
Land of Uz; Job's loss of children and wealth

D. **Scene IV,** Chapter 2:1-6
Heaven; God and Satan

E. **Scene V,** Chapter 2:7-10
Land of Uz; Job's loss of health and wife's sympathy

II.   DIALOGUE, Chapters 2:11—42:6
(Poetry)

A. **Scene VI,** Chapters 2:11–37:24
City Dump

1. Job's loss of understanding of friends, 2:11-13

2. Job vs. Eliphaz, Bildad, and Zophar, 3:1—32:1

3. Job vs. Elihu, 32:2—37:24

B. **Scene VII,** Chapters 38:1–42:6
Jehovah vs. Job

III.   EPILOGUE, Chapter 42:7-17
(Prose)
Scene VIII
Land of Uz; Job's blessings doubled

Psalms

THE BOOK OF WORSHIP
THE HYMN BOOK OF THE TEMPLE

TITLE: The title in Hebrew means *Praises* or *Book of Praises*. The title in the Greek suggests the idea of an instrumental accompaniment. Our title comes from the Greek *psalmos*.

WRITERS: Many writers contributed one or more psalms. They are as follows: David, 73; Moses, 1 (90th); Solomon, 2; Sons of Korah, 11; Asaph, 12; Heman, 1 (88th); Ethan, 1 (89th); Hezekiah, 10; "Orphanic," 39.

David, "the sweet psalmist of Israel" (2 Samuel 23:1), has 73 psalms assigned to him (Psalm 2 is ascribed to him in Acts 4:25; Psalm 95 in Hebrews 4:7). Also, he could be the author of some of the "Orphanic" psalms. He had a special aptitude for and was peculiarly endowed to write these songs from experience. He arranged those in existence in his day for temple use.

THEME: Christ (the Messiah) is prominent throughout (Luke 24:44). The King and the kingdom are the theme songs of the Psalms.

KEY WORD: Hallelujah

KEY PSALM: Psalm 150. "Hallelujah" occurs 13 times in six verses.

FEATURES: The Psalms record deep devotion, intense feeling, exalted emotion, and dark dejection. The Psalms play with all the stops pulled out upon the keyboard of the human soul. They run the psychological gamut. This book has been called the epitome and anatomy of the soul and designated as the garden of the Scriptures. The place Psalms have held in the lives of God's people testifies to their universality, although they have a peculiar Jewish application. They express the deep feelings of all believing hearts in all generations.

The Psalms are full of Christ. There is a more complete picture of Him in Psalms than in the Gospels. The Gospels tell us that He went to the mountain to pray, but the Psalms give us His prayer. The Gospels tell us that He was crucified, but the Psalms tell us what went on in His own heart during the crucifixion. The Gospels tell us He went back to heaven, but the Psalms begin where the Gospels leave off and show us Christ seated in heaven.

There are many types of psalms. Although all of them have Christ as the object of worship, some are technically called messianic psalms. These record the birth, life, death, resurrection, glory, priesthood, kingship, and return of Christ. The imprecatory psalms have caused the most criticism because of their vindictiveness and prayers for judgment. (Christians are told to love their enemies.) These psalms come from a time of war and from a people who, under law, were looking for justice and peace on the earth. They look to a time coming on the earth when the Antichrist will be in power. We have no reasonable basis to say how people should act and what they should say under those circumstances. Other types of psalms include penitential, historic, nature, pilgrim, Hallel, missionary, puritan, acrostic, and praise of God's Word.

OUTLINE: (Corresponds to Pentateuch of Moses)

I. **Genesis section,** Psalms 1–41
   Man in a state of blessedness, fall, and recovery (Man in View)

   - **Psalm 1:** Perfect Man (last Adam)
   - **Psalm 2:** Rebellious man
   - **Psalm 3:** Perfect Man rejected
   - **Psalm 4:** Conflict between Seed of woman and serpent
   - **Psalm 5:** Perfect Man in midst of enemies
   - **Psalm 6:** Perfect Man in midst of chastisement (bruising heel)
   - **Psalm 7:** Perfect Man in midst of false witnesses
   - **Psalm 8:** Repair of man comes through Man (bruising head)
   - **Psalms 9– 15:** Enemy and Antichrist conflict; final deliverance
   - **Psalms 16–41:** Christ in midst of His people, sanctifying them to God

II. **Exodus section,** Psalms 42–72
   Ruin and Redemption (Israel in View)

   - **Psalms 42–49:** Israel's ruin
   - **Psalms 50–60:** Israel's Redeemer
   - **Psalms 61–72:** Israel's redemption

III. **Leviticus section,** Psalms 73–89
   Darkness and Dawn (Sanctuary in View)

IV. **Numbers section,** Psalms 90–106
   Peril and Protection of Pilgrims (Earth in View)

V. **Deuteronomy section,** Psalms 107–150
   Perfection and Praise of the Word of God
   Psalm 119, an acrostic in the heart of this section, refers to the Word of God in almost every verse. It is the longest chapter in the Bible.

Proverbs

Proverbs

WRITER: Solomon is the writer of the next three books of the Bible: Proverbs, Ecclesiastes, and Song of Solomon. Proverbs is the book on wisdom; Ecclesiastes is the book on folly; Song of Solomon is the book on love. Love is the happy medium between wisdom and folly. Solomon is an authority on all three subjects (1 Kings 4:32-34).

KEY VERSE: Proverbs 1:7

DEFINITIONS: "A proverb is a saying that conveys a specific truth in a pointed, pithy way." "Proverbs are short sentences, drawn from long experience." A truth couched in a form that is easy to remember, a philosophy based on experience, and a rule for conduct. A proverb is a sententious sentence, a maxim, an old saying, an old saw, a bromide, and an epigram.

FEATURES: The Orient and ancient East are the home of proverbs. Evidently Solomon gathered together many from other sources. He was the editor of all and the author of some. Dr. Thirtle and other scholars noted that there is a change of pronoun in the book from the second person to the third person. Their conclusions are that the proverbs in the second person were taught to Solomon by his teachers, and the proverbs in the third person were composed by Solomon.

There is a difference between the book of Proverbs and proverbs in other writings (the Greeks were great at making proverbs, especially the gnostic poets):

1 Proverbs bear no unscientific statement or inaccurate observation; e.g., "Out of the heart proceed the issues of life" (see Proverbs 4:23); about 2700 years later, William Harvey found that the blood circulates. In contrast, in the Epistle of Barnabas (an apocryphal book) mention is made of the mythical phoenix, a bird that consumes itself by fire and then rises in resurrection. A fable such as this does not appear in the book of Proverbs, nor anywhere else in the Bible.

2 The Proverbs are on a high moral plane. The immoral sayings that occur in other writings are not present. Justin Martyr said that Socrates was a Christian before Christ. Although, according to his admirers, Socrates portrays a high conception of morals, he also gives instructions to harlots on how to conduct themselves. The best that can be said of him is that he was unmoral.

3 The Proverbs do not contradict, while man's proverbs are often in opposition to each other. For example: "Look before you leap" vs. "He who hesitates is lost." "A man gets no more than he pays for" vs. "The best things in life are free." "Leave well enough alone" vs. "Progress never stands still." "A rolling stone gathers no moss" vs. "A setting hen does not get fat."

Although the book of Proverbs seems to be a collection of sayings without any particular regard for orderly arrangement, the contrary is true. It is not a hodgepodge of unrelated statements, nor is it a discourse of cabbages and kings (Ecclesiastes 12:9). The book tells a story. It is a picture of a young man starting out in life. His first lesson is given in 1:7. Two schools bid for him and both send their literature. One is the school of Wisdom, the other is the school for fools. *Wisdom is none other than the Lord Jesus Christ* (see 1 Corinthians 1:30). In chapter 8, the young man goes to the academy of Wisdom where he is taught in proverbs. From chapters 10 through 24, the young man is in the classroom of Wisdom. The advice herein transcends all dispensations.

There is a proverb that is a thumbnail sketch of every character in the Bible (we can suggest only a few). Likewise, there is a proverb that will fit all your friends and acquaintances, which adds interest to the reading of the book (but may not increase your popularity if you identify them publicly).

Solomon wrote 3000 proverbs (1 Kings 4:32); we have fewer than 1000 of them in this book.

STRUCTURE OF PROVERBS, by A. C. Gaebelein:

The literary form of these proverbs is mostly in the form of couplets. The two clauses of the couplet are generally related to each other by what has been termed parallelism, according to Hebrew poetry. Three kinds of parallelism have been pointed out:

1 - *Synonymous Parallelism.* Here the second clause restates what is given in the first clause.	*Judgments are prepared for scoffers, and stripes for the back of fools.* (Proverbs 19:29)
2 - *Antithetic (Contrast) Parallelism.* Here a truth is stated in the first clause and made stronger in the second clause by contrast with an opposite truth.	*The light of the righteous rejoiceth: but the lamp of the wicked shall be put out.* (Proverbs 13:9)
3 - *Synthetic Parallelism.* The second clause develops the thought of the first.	*The fear of a king is like the roaring of a lion: whoso provoketh him to anger sinneth against his own soul.* (Proverbs 20:2)

OUTLINE:

I.   **Wisdom and folly contrasted,** Chapters 1—9

II. **Proverbs of Solomon, written and set in order by himself,** Chapters 10—24

III. **Proverbs of Solomon, set in order by men of Hezekiah,** Chapters 25—29

IV. **Oracle of Agur, unknown sage,** Chapter 30

V.   **Proverbs of a mother to Lemuel,** Chapter 31

Ecclesiastes

Ecclesiastes

WRITER: Solomon. The book is the "dramatic autobiography of his life when he got away from God."

TITLE: *Ecclesiastes* means "preacher" or "philosopher."

PURPOSE: The purpose of any book of the Bible is important to the correct understanding of it; this is no more evident than here. Human philosophy, apart from God, must inevitably reach the conclusions in this book; therefore, there are many statements which seem to contradict the remainder of Scripture. It almost frightens us to know that this book has been the favorite of atheists, and they (e.g., Volney and Voltaire) have quoted from it profusely. Man has tried to be happy without God, and this book shows the absurdity of the attempt. Solomon, the wisest of men, tried every field of endeavor and pleasure known to man; his conclusion was, "All is vanity."

God showed Job, a righteous man, that he was a sinner in God's sight. In Ecclesiastes God showed Solomon, the wisest man, that he was a fool in God's sight.

ESTIMATIONS: In Ecclesiastes, we learn that without Christ we cannot be satisfied, even if we possess the whole world—the heart is too large for the object. In the Song of Solomon, we learn that if we turn from the world and set our affections on Christ, we cannot fathom the infinite preciousness of His love—the Object is too large for the heart.

Dr. A. T. Pierson said, "There is a danger in pressing the words in the Bible into a positive announcement of scientific fact, so marvelous are some of these correspondencies. But it is certainly a curious fact that Solomon should use language entirely consistent with discoveries such as evaporation and storm currents (1:6, 7). Some have boldly said that Redfield's theory of storms is here explicitly stated. Without taking such ground, we ask, who taught Solomon to use terms that readily accommodate facts? Who taught him that the movement of the winds, which seem to be so lawless and uncertain, is ruled by laws as positive as those which rule the growth of the plant; and that by evaporation, the waters that fall on the earth are continually rising again, so that the sea never overflows? Ecclesiastes 12:6 is a poetic description of death. The 'silver cord' describes the spinal marrow, the 'golden bowl' the basin which holds the brain, the 'pitcher' the lungs, and the 'wheel' the heart. Without claiming that Solomon was inspired to foretell the circulation of the blood, 26 centuries before Harvey announced it, is it not remarkable that the language he uses exactly suits the facts—a wheel pumping up through one pipe to discharge through another?"

KEY WORD: "Vanity" occurs 37 times. Most Bible teachers would give the phrase "under the sun," which occurs 29 times.

OUTLINE:

I. **Problem stated: "All is vanity,"** Chapter 1:1-3

II. **Experiment made,** Chapters 1:4–12:12
   Seeking satisfaction in the following:

   A. Science (the laws of nature), Chapter 1:4-11

   B. Wisdom and philosophy, Chapter 1:12-18

   C. Pleasure, Chapter 2:1-11

   D. Materialism (living for the "now"), Chapter 2:12-26

   E. Fatalism, Chapter 3:1-15

   F. Egoism, Chapters 3:16–4:16

   G. Religion, Chapter 5:1-8

   H. Wealth, Chapters 5:9–6:12

   I. Morality (the "good life"), Chapters 7:1–12:12

III. **Result of experiment, Chapter 12:13, 14**
   All things under the sun are vanity.

A right relationship with God, in any age, through the way He has made, brings the only abiding satisfaction. *What a difference between the man "under the sun" and the man "in Christ" seated in the heavenlies far above all suns!*

Song of Solomon

Song of Solomon

WRITER:
Solomon (1:1). Solomon was the author of 1,005 songs (1 Kings 4:32), but we have only one (Song of Songs); as the name would indicate, it is the best.

KEY WORDS:
"Beloved," the name for Him; "love," the name for her.

KEY VERSES:
Song of Solomon 6:3 and 8:7

THE MEANING:
The Song of Solomon is a parabolic poem. The *interpretation*, not the inspiration, causes the difficulty—although there are some who actually feel it should not be in the Bible. Since it is in the canon of Scripture, it is the great neglected book of the Bible. Often young preachers are counseled not to use it until they become old men. The Jews called it the Holy of Holies of Scripture. Origen and Jerome tell us that the Jews would not permit their young men to read it until they were 30 years old. Surely any fragile flower requires delicate handling. There have been four different and important meanings found in this book:

1 It sets forth the glory of wedded love; declaring the sacredness of marital relationship and that marriage is a divine institution. To our occidental minds, it borders on the vulgar, but when it is compared to other oriental poetry, it is indeed tame and lacks the splash of color and extravagant terms which characterize oriental (e.g., Persian) poetry. The Jews taught that it sets forth the heart of a satisfied husband and a devoted wife.

2 It sets forth the love of Jehovah for Israel. The prophets spoke of Israel as the wife of Jehovah.

These two interpretations have been set forth by the scribes and rabbis of Israel and have been accepted by the church. However, there are two other interpretations:

3 It is a picture of Christ and the church. The church is the bride of Christ, a familiar figure of Scripture (2 Corinthians 11:2; Ephesians 5:27; Revelation 21).

4 It depicts the communion of Christ and the individual believer. The soul's communion with Christ is here set forth.

"The Song of Solomon tests the spiritual capacity of the reader."

STORY OUTLINE: Since this book is a series of scenes in a drama that is not told in chronological sequence, we shall make no attempt to outline the book.

The popular interpretation, that it tells the story of a girl kidnapped by Solomon, is repugnant. The book of Dr. H. A. Ironside is especially recommended, as it contains the only adequate and satisfying interpretation that I have seen. The key to the story is found in 8:11. The story is of a poor family of Ephraim in which there is a girl who is a sort of Cinderella. The poverty of the family forces her into the vineyards where she meets the young shepherd. The story of their love is first told. Then he leaves her with the promise that he will return. He is absent for a long time, and she despairs of his return. One day, the electrifying word is shouted along the way that King Solomon is coming by. She is not interested and takes no further notice until word is brought to her that King Solomon wants to see her. She is puzzled until she is brought into his presence where she recognizes him as her shepherd lover. He takes her to his palace in Jerusalem where most of the song takes place.

COMMENT: The setting of the drama is the palace in Jerusalem, and some of the scenes are flashbacks to a previous time. There is a reminder here of the Greek drama where a chorus talks back and forth to the protagonists of the play. The daughters of Jerusalem carry along the tempo of the story. Some of these dialogues were evidently to be sung. Several lovely scenes are introduced at Jerusalem which find a counterpart in the church.

When reading the Song of Solomon, take off the shoes from the natural man, for the ground on which you stand is spiritual ground.

Isaiah

Prophetic Books

Beginning with Isaiah, and continuing through the Old Testament, there is a section of Scripture called the prophetic portion of the Bible. Although the predictive element bulks large in this section, the prophets were more than fortune-tellers. Actually, they were men raised up of God in a decadent day when both priest and king were no longer worthy channels through whom the expressions of God might flow.

These men not only spoke of events in the far-off future but also spoke of local events in the immediate future. They had to speak in this manner in order to qualify for this office under God, according to the Mosaic code (Deuteronomy 18:20-22).

If the local event did not transpire just as the prophet predicted, he was labeled a false prophet and was so treated. You may be sure that the message of the false prophet is not in the library of inspired Scripture. The prophetic books are filled with events that are local and fulfilled. A sharp distinction needs to be drawn between this portion and that which is yet to be fulfilled.

One of the greatest evidences of the fact that these men were speaking the words of God is revealed in the hundreds of prophecies that have been fulfilled literally. Man cannot guess the future. Even the meteorologists have difficulty in prognosticating the weather 24 hours in advance, although they have the advantage of all sorts of scientific and mechanical devices to assist them. No modern weather forecaster could have been an accepted prophet in Israel! The law of compound probability forbids man from consistently foretelling the future. Each uncertain element added decreases the chance of accuracy by 50%. The example of hundreds of prophecies literally fulfilled has a genuine appeal to the honest mind and sincere seeker after the truth. Fulfilled prophecy is one of the infallible proofs of plenary, verbal inspiration of Scripture.

The predictive element is the peculiar and particular contribution of these men of God. This does not mean there was not this element before them or after them. The last book of the Bible closes the message of God for the future.

The prophets were extremely nationalistic. They rebuked sin in high as well as low places. They warned the nation. They pleaded with a proud people to humble themselves and return to God. Fire and tears were mingled in their message, which was not one of doom and gloom alone, for they saw the Day of the Lord and the glory to follow. All of them looked through the darkness to the dawn of a new day. In the night of sin they saw the light of a coming Savior and Sovereign; they saw the millennial kingdom coming in all its fullness. Their message must be interpreted before an appreciation of the kingdom in the New Testament can be attained. The correct perspective of the kingdom must be gained through the eye of the Old Testament prophets. The prophets were not supermen—they were men of like passions as we are, but having spoken for God, their message is still the infallible and inspired Word of God (1 Peter 1:10, 11 and 2 Peter 1:19-21).

Sweet is the harp of prophecy; too sweet not to be wronged by a mere mortal touch.
— William Cowper

WRITER: Isaiah gives us very little of an historical character concerning himself. There are a few scant references to his life and ministry. In Isaiah 1:1 he gives "the days" in which his lot was cast. It was during the reigns of "Uzziah, Jotham, Ahaz, and Hezekiah, kings of Judah." These were not the darkest days in Judah internally. Uzziah and Hezekiah were enlightened rulers who sought to serve God. But the days were extremely dark because of the menace of the formidable kingdom of Assyria in the north. The northern kingdom of Israel was carried away into captivity during this period.

Isaiah 6 records the personal call and commission of Isaiah. This chapter should come first in the prophecy—logically if not chronologically. Isaiah 36—39 is the historical section, which records the ministry of Isaiah during the crisis when the Assyrian host encompassed Jerusalem. Beyond these few personal sections, Isaiah stands in the shadow as he points to another Person who is coming.

It is stated by some that Isaiah belonged to the royal family of David. This cannot be positively affirmed. Likewise, it has been stated that he is referred to in Hebrews 11:37 as the one "sawn asunder." This may or may not be true. The liberal critic has sawn him asunder in forging the fake fabric of the Deutero-Isaiah hypothesis. Some have gone so far as to fabricate a Trito-Isaiah. There is not a scrap of documentary evidence beyond the skepticism of the destructive critic. They have cut Isaiah up like a railroad restaurant pie. History presents only one Isaiah, not two or three.

THEME: As the New Testament presents the Lord Jesus Christ as its theme, so Isaiah presents the Lord Jesus Christ as his theme. Isaiah has been called the fifth evangelist; the book of Isaiah has been called the fifth Gospel. Christ's virgin birth, His character, His life, His death, His resurrection, and His second coming are all presented in Isaiah with definiteness and clarity.

OUTLINE:

I. **Judgment (poetry),** Chapters 1–35
    Revelation of the Sovereign on the throne.
    (The Crown, chapter 6. The government of God.)

    A. Solemn call to the universe to come into the courtroom to hear God's charge against the nation Israel, Chapter 1

    B. Preview of the future for Judah and Jerusalem, Chapter 2

    C. Present view of Judah and Jerusalem, Chapter 3

    D. Another preview of the future, Chapter 4

    E. Parable of the vineyard and woes predicted on Israel, Chapter 5

    F. Isaiah's personal call and commission as prophet, Chapter 6

    G. Prediction of local and far events, Chapters 7–10
       (Hope of future in coming Child)

    H. Millennial kingdom, Chapters 11, 12

    I. Burdens of surrounding nations (largely fulfilled), Chapters 13–23

        1. Burden of Babylon, Chapters 13, 14

        2. Burden of Moab, Chapters 15, 16

        3. Burden of Damascus, Chapter 17

        4. Burden of the land beyond the rivers of Ethiopia, Chapter 18

    5. Burden of Egypt, Chapters 19, 20

    6. Burden of Babylon, Edom, Arabia, Chapter 21

    7. Burden of the Valley of Vision, Chapter 22

    8. Burden of Tyre, Chapter 23

J. Kingdom, process and program by which the throne is established on earth, Chapters 24–34

K. Kingdom, mundane blessings of the Millennium, Chapter 35

II. Historic interlude (prose), Chapters 36–39
(This section is probably a prophetic picture of how God will deliver His people in the Great Tribulation [see 2 Kings 18, 19 and 2 Chronicles 29, 30].)

A. King Hezekiah and the invasion of Sennacherib, king of Assyria, Chapter 36

B. King Hezekiah's prayer and the destruction of the Assyrian hosts, Chapter 37

C. King Hezekiah's sickness, prayer and healing, Chapter 38

D. King Hezekiah plays the fool, Chapter 39

III. Salvation (poetry), Chapters 40–66
Revelation of the Savior in the place of suffering.
(The Cross, chapter 53. The grace of God. *There is a three-fold division marked by the concluding thought in each division, "There is no peace to the wicked."*)

A. Comfort of Jehovah which comes through the Servant, Chapters 40–48
(Polemic against idolatry–help and hope come only through the Servant.)

B. Salvation of Jehovah which comes through the suffering Servant, Chapters 49–57

    1. Redeemer of the whole world, who is God's Servant, Chapters 49:1— 52:12

    2. Redemption wrought by the suffering Servant, who is God's Sheep (Lamb), Chapters 52:13—53:12

    3. Results of the redemption wrought by the Redeemer, who is God's only Savior, Chapters 54—57

C. Glory of Jehovah which comes through the suffering Servant, Chapters 58–66

    1. Sin hinders the manifestation of the glory of God, Chapters 58, 59

    2. Redeemer is coming to Zion, Chapters 60—66
(Nothing can hinder God's progress—He will judge sin.)

Jeremiah

Jeremiah

WRITER: Jeremiah, "the prophet of the broken heart"

HIS LIFE: His book is partly autobiographical since he gave us so much of his personal history.

1 – Born a priest in Anathoth, north of Jerusalem (1:1).

2 – Chosen to be a prophet before he was born (1:5).

3 – Called to the prophetic office while very young (1:6).

4 – Commissioned (1:9, 10).

5 – Began his ministry during the reign of King Josiah and was a mourner at his funeral (2 Chronicles 35:25).

6 – Forbidden to marry because of the terrible times (16:1-4).

7 – Never made a convert, and was rejected by his people (11:18-21; 12:6; 18:18), hated, beaten, put in stocks (20:1-3), imprisoned (37:11-16), and charged with being a traitor.

8 – His message broke his own heart (9:1).

9 – Wanted to resign but could not (20:9).

10 - He saw the destruction of Jerusalem and the Babylonian captivity, and was permitted to remain in the land by the captain of the Babylonian forces. When the remnant wanted to flee to Egypt, Jeremiah prophesied against it (42:15-43:3), was forced to go with the remnant to Egypt (43:6, 7), and died there. Tradition says that he was stoned by the remnant.

HIS PERSONALITY: God chose this man, who had a mother's heart, a trembling voice, and tear-filled eyes, to deliver a harsh message of judgment. The message that he gave broke his own heart.

One author has written, "He was not a man mighty as Elijah, eloquent as Isaiah, or seraphic as Ezekiel, but one who was timid and shrinking, conscious of his helplessness, yearning for a sympathy and love he was never to know—such was the chosen organ through which the Word of the Lord came to that corrupt and degenerate age."

The Lord Jesus Christ, weeping over Jerusalem, was a perfect fulfillment of Jeremiah.

HIS MESSAGE: The message of Jeremiah was the most unwelcome ever delivered to a people. He was called a traitor because he said that they were to yield to Babylon (34; 38:17-23). Isaiah, almost a century before him, had said to resist. Why this change? In Jeremiah's day there was only one thing left to do—surrender. In the economy of God the nation was through (15:1), and the "times of the Gentiles" had already begun with Babylon, the head of gold (cf. Daniel 2).

Jeremiah predicted the 70-year captivity in Babylon (25:9-12). However, he saw beyond the darkness to the light, and no prophet spoke so glowingly of the future as did he (23:3-8; 30; 31; 33:15-22).

The message of Jeremiah was not only unwelcomed, but it was rejected by the nation (26:8-16).

KEY WORDS:

Backsliding—occurs 13 times (used only four other times in the Old Testament [Proverbs once, Hosea three times])

Babylon—occurs 164 times (more than in the rest of Scripture combined)

OUTLINE: (Difficult to outline because there is no logical or chronological order)

I. **Call of prophet during reign of Josiah,** Chapter 1

II. **Prophecies to Judah and Jerusalem prior to Zedekiah's reign,** Chapters 2—20

   A. Twofold condemnation of Judah, Chapters 2—3:5

      1. Rejected Jehovah

      2. Reared their own gods

   B. Charge of backsliding during reign of Josiah, Chapters 3:6—6:30

   C. Warning delivered in the gate of the Lord's house, Chapters 7—10

   D. Israel disobeyed God's covenant made in wilderness, Chapters 11, 12

   E. Parable in action—the linen girdle, Chapter 13

   F. Backsliding nation judged by drought and famine, Chapters 14, 15

   G. Jeremiah forbidden to marry, Chapters 16—17:18

   H. Message to king in the gate, Chapter 17:19-27

   I. Sign at the potter's house, Chapters 18, 19

   J. Jeremiah's persecution, Chapter 20

III. **Prophecies during reign of Zedekiah,** Chapters 21—29
    (Leads to destruction of Jerusalem)

   A. Answer to Zedekiah re: Nebuchadnezzar, Chapters 21, 22

   B. A bright light in a very dark day, Chapter 23

   C. Parable of two baskets of figs, Chapter 24

   D. God spells out 70-year captivity, Chapter 25

   E. Message in temple court during reign of Jehoiakim, Chapter 26

   F. Parable of the yokes, Chapters 27, 28

   G. Message of hope to first delegation of captives, Chapter 29

IV. **Prophecies re: future of 12 tribes and Judah's near captivity,** Chapters 30—39

   A. Coming of Great Tribulation, Chapter 30

   B. The "I will" chapter, Chapter 31

   C. Jeremiah imprisoned, buys real estate, Chapter 32

   D. Coming kingdom as promised to David, Chapter 33

E. Zedekiah's captivity foretold, Chapter 34

F. Rechabites obey God, Chapter 35

G. Jehoiakim destroys Word of God with knife and fire, Chapter 36

H. Jeremiah imprisoned again, Chapters 37, 38

I. Judah goes into captivity; Jeremiah released from prison, Chapter 39

V. **Prophecies to remnant left in land after destruction of Jerusalem, Chapters 40–42**

VI. **Prophecies during Jeremiah's last days in Egypt, Chapters 43–51**

A. To remnant in Egypt, Chapters 43, 44

B. To Baruch, Chapter 45

C. To Egypt, Chapter 46

D. To Philistia, Chapter 47

E. To Moab, Chapter 48

F. To Ammon, Edom, Damascus, Kedar, Hazor and Elam, Chapter 49

G. To Babylon, Chapters 50, 51

VII. **Fulfillment of prophesied destruction of Jerusalem, Chapter 52**

Lamentations

Lamentations

WRITER: Jeremiah

ESTIMATION: "There is nothing like the Lamentations of Jeremiah in the whole world. There has been plenty of sorrow in every age, and in every land, but such another preacher and author, with such a heart for sorrow, has never again been born. Dante comes next to Jeremiah, and we know that Jeremiah was the great exile's favorite prophet." (Whyte)

The book is filled with tears and sorrow. It is a paean of pain, a poem of pity, a proverb of pathos, a hymn of heartbreak, a psalm of sadness, a symphony of sorrow, a story of sifting, a tale of tears, a dirge of desolation, a tragedy of travail, an account of agony, and a book of "boo-hoo." It is the wailing wall of the Bible.

KEY VERSE: Lamentations 1:18 explains the reason that Jerusalem is in ruins.

FEATURE: Jeremiah reminds us of Another as He sat weeping over Jerusalem. The only difference is that Jerusalem was in ruins and the temple burned as Jeremiah gazed upon the debris. Jesus, about six centuries later, wept over the city because it would be destroyed again in the near future.

To Jeremiah, the destruction of Jerusalem was a matter of history. To Jesus, the destruction of Jerusalem was a matter of prophecy. No blues singer ever sang a sadder song than Jeremiah. Lamentations is composed of five of his sad songs, which are elegies.

OUTLINE:

I. Elegy, Chapter 1
A call to consider the destruction of Jerusalem.
vv. 8, 18—The reason for the frightful destruction.
v. 12—An invitation to all to enter into the sorrow of the prophet.

II. Elegy, Chapter 2
v. 10—Doleful details of the effect of the judgment of God upon the remnant that remain.
v. 15—The elation of the enemy from without.

III. Elegy, Chapter 3
The tragic and catastrophic destruction of Jerusalem would have been total had it not been for the mercies and faithfulness of God.

IV. Elegy, Chapter 4
Contrast between the former state of prosperity and the present state of Jerusalem in poverty.

V. Elegy, Chapter 5
A cry to God to remember the nation Israel. "Prayer of Jeremiah."

Ezekiel

Ezekiel

WRITER: Ezekiel was a priest (Ezekiel 1:3) but never served in that office, as he was still a young man when he was taken captive during the reign of Jehoiachin (2 Kings 24:10-16). Daniel was taken captive in the first captivity during Jehoiakim's reign, about eight years before Ezekiel was taken captive.

Ezekiel was contemporary with Jeremiah and Daniel. Jeremiah was an old man who spoke to the remnant that remained in the land; Daniel spoke in the court of the king of Babylon; Ezekiel spoke to the captives who had been brought to the rivers of Babylon. While the other captives wept when they remembered Zion, Ezekiel exulted in the greatest visions ever given to any prophet.

HIS MESSAGE: His message was the most spiritual of the prophets, as he dealt more with the person of God. Someone has said, "Ezekiel is the prophet of the Spirit, as Isaiah is the prophet of the Son, and Jeremiah the prophet of the Father."

During the first years of the captivity, the false prophets said that the people would be returned to Jerusalem and that the city would not be destroyed. It was not until the final deportation, during Zedekiah's reign, that the city was destroyed—some 11 years after Ezekiel was taken captive.

Jeremiah had sent a message to Babylon (Jeremiah 29) saying that the city would be destroyed. Ezekiel confirmed this message and warned the people that they must turn to God before they could return to Jerusalem.

Ezekiel began his ministry five years after his captivity, when he was about 30 years old.

HIS METHOD: In many ways he spoke in the darkest days of the nation. He stood at the bottom of the valley in the darkest corner. He had to meet the false hope given by the false prophets and the indifference and the despondency begotten in the days of sin and disaster. The people would not listen to him or his message. Therefore, he resorted to a new method. Instead of speaking in parables, he acted them out (Ezekiel 24:24). We have had "flagpole sitters" and "walkathons" in our day, which attract the attention of the public. This sort of thing was the method of Ezekiel and is indicative of a day of decay.

HIS MEANING: Ezekiel was the prophet of the glory of the Lord. Three prophets of Israel spoke when they were out of the land: Ezekiel, Daniel, and John. Each wrote an apocalypse. Although they used highly symbolic language, they saw the brightest light and held the highest hope. Ezekiel saw the Shekinah glory of the Lord leave Solomon's temple, and he saw the return of the glory of the Lord which was projected into the future during the kingdom. The meaning of Ezekiel is seen in the coming glory during the kingdom. Ezekiel looked beyond the sufferings of Christ to "the glory that should follow" (1 Peter 1:11).

OUTLINE:

I. **Glory of the Lord; commission of the prophet,** Chapters 1–7

   A. Display of the glory, Chapter 1

   B. Prophet's call and endowment with power for the office, Chapter 2

   C. Prophet's preparation; office as watchman, Chapter 3

   D. Judgment of Jerusalem, Chapter 4

   E. Sign of prophet shaving hair, Chapter 5

   F. Sword to fall upon Jerusalem; remnant to be saved, Chapter 6

   G. Prophecy of final destruction of Jerusalem, Chapter 7

II. **Glory of the Lord; complete captivity of Jerusalem and Israel; departure of the glory,** Chapters 8–24

  A. Vision of the glory; temple defilement by idolatry explains its destruction, Chapter 8

  B. Shekinah glory prepares to leave temple, Chapter 9

  C. Shekinah glory fills holy place; leaves the temple, Chapter 10

  D. Prophecy against rulers of Jerusalem, Chapter 11

  E. Ezekiel enacts destruction of Jerusalem, Chapter 12

  F. Prophecy against pseudo-prophets and prophetesses, Chapter 13

  G. Prophecy against idolatry of elders; certain destruction of Jerusalem, Chapter 14

  H. Vision of the vine, Chapter 15

  I. Jerusalem likened to abandoned baby adopted by God, Chapter 16

  J. Riddle of two eagles, Chapter 17

  K. Wages of sin is death; Jerusalem is the awful example, Chapter 18

  L. Elegy of Jehovah over princes of Israel, Chapter 19

  M. Review of Israel's long history of sins; future judgment and restoration, Chapter 20

  N. King of Babylon to remove last king of Davidic line until Messiah comes, Chapter 21

  O. Review of abominations of Jerusalem, Chapter 22

  P. Parable of two sisters—Oholah (Samaria) and Oholibah (Jerusalem), Chapter 23

  Q. Parable of the boiling pot, Chapter 24

III. **Glory of the Lord; judgment of nations,** Chapters 25–32

  A. Against Ammon, Moab, Edom, Philistia, Chapter 25

  B. Against Tyre, Chapters 26–28

  C. Against Egypt, Chapters 29–32

IV. **Glory of the Lord and coming kingdom,** Chapters 33–48

  A. Re-commission of the prophet, Chapters 33, 34

  B. Restoration of Israel, Chapters 35, 36

  C. Resurrection of Israel, Chapter 37

  D. Repudiation of Gog and Magog, Chapters 38, 39

  E. Rebuilt temple, Chapters 40–42

  F. Return of the glory of the Lord, Chapters 43–48

Daniel

Daniel

BACKGROUND: The book of Daniel has been the battlefield between conservative and liberal scholars for years. The heat of battle is now past— with each side claiming a major victory. However, the very fact that the book of Daniel remains intact in Scripture and that the early dating of this book (the sixth century B.C.) has been maintained successfully by conservative scholars against the massed onslaught of arrogant liberalism, is in itself a valid argument for the original and conservative position.

It is not in the purview of these brief notes to enter into useless argument and fight again about that which has been already won. We accept the findings of conservative scholarship—that the man Daniel was not a deceiver and that his book was not a forgery. Our Lord called the Pharisees "hypocrites," but He called Daniel "the prophet." He has never reversed this arrangement, and the endorsement of the Lord Jesus Christ is valid and sufficient for every believer whether or not he has examined the arguments of the critics. It satisfies the sincere saint without his having studied the answers of conservative scholarship (see Hebrews 11:33).

WRITER: We know more of Daniel the man than we do of any other prophet. He gave us a personal account of his life from the time he was carried captive to Babylon in the third year of the reign of Jehoiakim, which was about 606 B.C. (Daniel 1:1), until the first year of King Cyrus, which was about 536 B.C. (Daniel 1:21 and also 9:2). Daniel's life and ministry bridged the entire 70 years of captivity. At the beginning of the book he is a boy in his teens, and at the end he is an old man of fourscore or more years.

Here is God's estimate of the man: "O Daniel, a man greatly beloved" (Daniel 10:11).

There are three words that characterize Daniel's life: purpose, prayer, and prophecy.

DATE: As previously indicated, we hold to the early date of the book of Daniel—between the third year of the reign of Nebuchadnezzar, about 606 B.C. and the first year of Cyrus, about 536 B.C.

HIS MESSAGE: Daniel was the prophet of "the times of the Gentiles" (see Luke 21:24). The major portion of his prophecies were directly concerned with the gentile nations. The notable exception is Daniel 9, which concerns the 70 weeks, but here the emphasis is upon the interval after the cutting off of the Messiah between the 69th week and the 70th week. It is during this period that the city and sanctuary are destroyed, and "the times of the Gentiles" are identified as the time when "Jerusalem shall be trodden down of the Gentiles" (Luke 21:24). Evidently, the "wise men from the east" knew the prophecy of Daniel. A portion of the book of Daniel was written in Aramaic, the language of the Gentiles of that day. All this does not imply that the book of Daniel was not written for the nation Israel; on the contrary, Israel was acquainted with the prophecies of Daniel in his day. Ezekiel, who was with the captives, made reference to the character of Daniel and to his office as a prophet (Ezekiel 14:14, 20; 28:3).

THEME: Daniel 2:44

Dr. G. Campbell Morgan gave this theme: "Persistent Government of God in the Government of the World." This is the book of the universal sovereignty of God. Prophecy is interwoven with history to show that God is overruling the idolatry, blasphemy, self-will, and intolerance of the Gentiles.

OUTLINE:

The Old Testament is written in the Hebrew language, with but one exception—a portion of the book of Daniel. From chapter 2, verse 4, through chapter 7, Daniel is in Aramaic, the Gentile and diplomatic language of Daniel's day. This section deals exclusively with "the times of the Gentiles." The remainder of the book correlates the nation Israel with this program. The book of Daniel deals with Gentiles and Jews—the church is totally excluded. This book is first to the Gentiles but also to the Jews.

THE BOOK OF DANIEL PROBABLY SHOULD BE DIVIDED AT THREE GOD-GIVEN BREAKS:

Personal history of Daniel, Chapters 1:1–2:3

Prophetic history of Daniel relating to gentile nations, Chapters 2:4–7:28

Prophecies relating to the nation Israel, Chapters 8:1–12:13

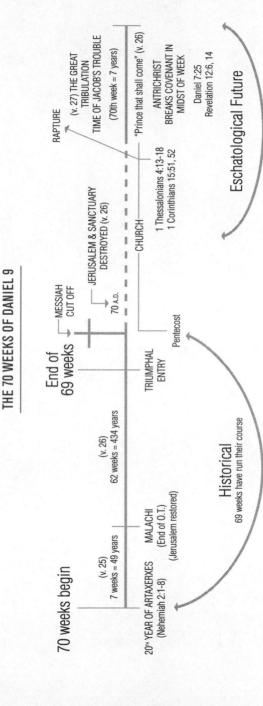

THE 70 WEEKS OF DANIEL 9

70 weeks begin

End of 69 weeks

RAPTURE

(v. 27) THE GREAT TRIBULATION
TIME OF JACOB'S TROUBLE
(70th week = 7 years)

"Prince that shall come" (v. 26)

ANTRICHRIST
BREAKS COVENANT IN
MIDST OF WEEK

Daniel 7:25
Revelation 12:6, 14

Eschatological Future

MESSIAH
CUT OFF

JERUSALEM & SANCTUARY
DESTROYED (v. 26)

70 A.D.

CHURCH

1 Thessalonians 4:13-18
1 Corinthians 15:51, 52

Pentecost

TRIUMPHAL
ENTRY

(v. 26)
62 weeks = 434 years

(v. 25)
7 weeks = 49 years

MALACHI
(End of O.T.)
(Jerusalem restored)

20TH YEAR OF ARTAXERXES
(Nehemiah 2:1-8)

Historical
69 weeks have run their course

(See Sir Robert Anderson's *The Coming Prince: The Last Great Monarch of Christendom*)

Hosea

Minor Prophets

Beginning with Hosea and concluding with Malachi, there are 12 short prophecies called the Minor Prophets. They are so called because of the size of the books and not because of their content. The Minor Prophets all deal with the same major issues of the Major Prophets. They are actually quoted by the Major Prophets (Jeremiah 26:18). The writers of the Minor Prophets were exceedingly nationalistic, but they were not isolationists. There were to be no godless alliances with other nations, but they were warned of an isolationism from God. They were extremely patriotic and denounced political and moral corruption. This has given rise to the modern emphasis on the social message of the prophets.

It is a striking fact that there is scant material on the Minor Prophets. A cursory inspection of any religious library will corroborate this. There is a wealth of material on most of the books of the Bible, but when you leave Daniel and pass over to Hosea, it is like going from a fertile valley to a sterile desert.

WRITER: Hosea. All that is known of him is what he reveals in his prophecy.

TIME: Hosea 1:1

In spite of the fact that Hosea mentions the four kings of Judah first and the one king of Israel last, he was a prophet to the northern kingdom, as the content of the book reveals. He was contemporary with Amos, another prophet to Israel, and also contemporary with Micah and Isaiah, prophets to Judah. His ministry extended over half a century, and he lived to see the fulfillment of his prophecy in the captivity of Israel.

THEME: "Return unto the LORD" (Hosea 6:1).

"Return" occurs 15 times.

"Ephraim" occurs 36 times.

"Backsliding" occurs three times. Hosea and Jeremiah are the two prophets who talk about backsliding and the cure for it.

What Jeremiah was to Judah at the time of the captivity of the southern kingdom, Hosea was to Israel, over a century before, at the time of the captivity of the northern kingdom. Both spoke out of a heartbreaking personal experience.

PERSONAL EXPERIENCE: Hosea's experience was in the home; Jeremiah's was in the nation. Jeremiah was commanded not to marry; Hosea was commanded to marry a harlot or, as he brutally stated the case, "a wife of whoredoms" (Hosea 1:2). He married Gomer, and she bore him two sons and a daughter. Afterward she played the harlot again, and Hosea put her out of his home. But God commanded him to take again this unfaithful harlot, to bring her back into his home, and to love her again. In effect, God said to Hosea, "Now you are prepared to speak for Me to Israel—Israel has played the harlot, but I love her and will yet bring her back into her homeland."

OUTLINE:

I.   **PERSONAL—The prophet and his faithless wife, Gomer,** Chapters 1–3

A. Marriage of Hosea and Gomer, the harlot, Chapter 1

B. Gomer proves faithless; Israel proves faithless; God proves faithful, Chapter 2

C. Hosea commanded to take Gomer again, Chapter 3

II. **PROPHETIC—The Lord and the faithless nation Israel,** Chapters 4–14

A. Israel plays the harlot, Chapters 4, 5

1. Israel guilty of lawlessness, immorality, ignorance of God's Word, and idolatry, Chapter 4

2. Israel turns from God; God turns from Israel; deterioration within follows, Chapter 5

B. Israel (Ephraim) will return in the last days; presently to be judged for current sins, Chapter 6

C. Israel (Ephraim) could escape judgment by turning to God who loves her (**key, 11:8**), Chapters 7–12

1. Israel (silly dove) turns to Egypt and Assyria, Chapter 7

2. Israel turns to golden calves and altars of sin, Chapter 8

3. Israel (backsliding heifer) turns to land productivity; will be driven from the land, Chapters 9, 10

4. Israel turns from God—must be judged; God will not give her up, Chapters 11, 12

D. Israel (Ephraim) will turn from idols to God in the last days, Chapters 13, 14

1. Israel will be judged in the present, Chapter 13

2. Israel will be saved in the future, Chapter 14

Joel

Joel

WRITER: Joel. Nothing is known of this prophet excpt what is given in the opening verse. His name means *Jehovah is God.*

TIME: Considered by many to be the earliest of the writing prophets, he was a prophet to Judah probably about the time of the reign of Joash, king of Judah. He probably knew Elijah and Elisha. The critical school, adopting their usual custom, have placed this book at the other extreme, even after the captivity.

THEME: "The day of the LORD"
(Joel 1:15; 2:1, 2, 10, 11, 30, 31; 3:14-16)

FEATURES:

1 "The day of the LORD" or "the day of Jehovah" is an expression introduced by Joel (if he is the first of the writing prophets—there are about 50 prophets in all). From the mountaintop of the beginning of written prophecy, he saw the farthest into the future. "The day of the LORD" is an expression that is fraught with meaning. It seems to include not only the coming Millennial Kingdom, but also to include all the judgments which precede the setting up of the Kingdom and the return of Christ.

2 His description of a literal plague of locusts and its comparison with future judgments is a dramatic and literary gem.

3 He is the prophet who mentioned the outpouring of the Holy Spirit, which was referred to by Peter on the Day of Pentecost.

OUTLINE:

I.   **Literal and local plague of locusts,** Chapter 1:1-14

II. **Looking to the day of the LORD (prelude),** Chapters 1:15–2:3

III. **Looking at the day of the LORD (postlude),** Chapter 3

   A. The Great Tribulation, vv. 1-15

   B. The Millennial Kingdom, vv. 16-21

Amos

Amos

WRITER: Amos was not a graduate of the school of the prophets but was a layman. He was a herdsman and a gatherer of sycamore fruit (Amos 1:1; 7:14, 15). He was a native of Tekoa (Amos 1:1), a village about 12 miles south of Jerusalem. Although born in Judea, his messages were to the northern kingdom of Israel primarily, and to the world in general, as the text indicates.

TIME: His ministry was during the reign of Jeroboam II, king of Israel, and Uzziah, king of Judah. He was a contemporary of Hosea in Israel and of Isaiah and Micah in Judah. The exact time was "two years before the earthquake" (Amos 1:1). This earthquake was of such proportions that Zechariah mentioned it 200 years later (Zechariah 14:5) and identified it as having come during the reign of Uzziah.

THEME: Amos presented God as the ruler of the world and declared that all nations were responsible to Him. The measure of responsibility is created by the light that a nation has. The final test for any nation (or individual) is found in Amos 3:3: "Can two walk together, except they be agreed?" In a day of prosperity, he pronounced punishment. Judgment of God awaited nations living in luxury and lolling in immorality.

OUTLINE:

I. Judgment on surrounding nations, Chapters 1:1–2:3

    A. Introduction, Chapter 1:1, 2

    B. Judgment against Syria for cruelty, Chapter 1:3-5

    C. Judgment against Philistia for making slaves, Chapter 1:6-8

    D. Judgment against Phoenicia for breaking treaty (selling slaves), Chapter 1:9, 10

    E. Judgment against Edom for revengeful spirit, Chapter 1:11, 12

    F. Judgment against Ammon for violent crimes, Chapter 1:13-15

    G. Judgment against Moab for injustice, Chapter 2:1-3

II. Judgment on Judah and Israel, Chapters 2:4–6:14

    A. Judgment against Judah for despising the Law, Chapter 2:4, 5

    B. Judgment against Israel for immorality and blasphemy, Chapter 2:6-16

    C. God's charge against whole house of Israel (12 tribes), Chapter 3
       (Privilege creates responsibility; the higher the blessing, the greater the punishment.)

    D. Israel punished in past for iniquity, Chapter 4

    E. Israel will be punished in future for iniquity, Chapter 5

    F. Israel admonished in present to depart from iniquity, Chapter 6

III. Visions of the future, Chapters 7–9

    A. Vision of grasshoppers, Chapter 7:1-3

    B. Vision of fire, Chapter 7:4-6

    C. Vision of plumbline, Chapter 7:7-9

    D. Historic interlude, Chapter 7:10-17
       (Personal experience of prophet)

    E. Vision of basket of summer fruit, Chapter 8

    F. Vision of worldwide dispersion, Chapter 9:1-10

    G. Vision of worldwide regathering and restoration of kingdom, 9:11-15

Obadiah

Obadiah

WRITER: Obadiah means *Servant of Jehovah.* He is one of four prophets about whom we know absolutely nothing, except that he wrote prophecy. The other three prophets are Habakkuk, Haggai, and Malachi. Obadiah is like a ghostwriter—he is there, but we do not know him. He lived up to his name. A servant boasts of no genealogy, neither exploits nor experiences. Dr. Edward Pusey said, "God has willed that his name alone and this brief prophecy should be known to the world."

DATE: There is a great difference of opinion as to the date of this prophet. There are some who give the date of 887 B.C., which fixes the time during the reign of Jehoram and the bloody Athaliah (cf. 2 Kings 8:18 with 11:1-16). Dr. Pusey placed him during the reign of Jehoshaphat (2 Chronicles 17:7). If this is accurate, we have one isolated reference to Obadiah in history. Nevertheless, this name was as common in that day as the name John is today. Canon Farrar gave the date as 587 B.C. Dr. William Moorehead concurred in this, as he suggested that Obadiah was probably a contemporary of Jeremiah. The whole question seems to hinge on verse 11. Is this verse historical or prophetical? The natural interpretation is the historic one, which would give it the late date. Most likely it was written subsequent to the Babylonian captivity.

KEY: Edom (Obadiah 1:6)

FEATURES: Obadiah is the shortest book in the Old Testament—only 21 verses. But the brevity of the message does not render it less important or less significant for us today. Like the other Minor Prophets, the message is primary, it is pertinent, it is practical, and it is poignant. It is a message that can be geared into this day in which we are living.

Obadiah tells us immediately, bluntly, and to the point, "Thus saith the LORD GOD concerning Edom ...." It is the prophecy of judgment against Edom.

BACKGROUND: The Edomites were those who were descended from Esau, just as the Israelites are those who are descended from Jacob.

The story of Esau and Jacob is that of twin brothers, sons of Isaac and Rebekah. They were not identical twins; actually they were opposites (see Genesis 25:24-34).

Esau despised his birthright. The man who had the birthright was in contact with God—he was the priest of his family, he was the man who had a covenant from God, the man who had a relationship with God. In effect Esau said, "I would rather have a bowl of soup than have a relationship with God."

Having seen Esau in the first book of the Old Testament, look now at the last book of the Old Testament and read this strange language:

I have loved you, saith the LORD. Yet ye say, Wherein hast thou loved us? Was not Esau Jacob's brother? saith the LORD: yet I loved Jacob, and I hated Esau .... (Malachi 1:2, 3)

This is a strange thing for God to say—"I loved Jacob, and I hated Esau." The explanation is in the little book of Obadiah.

OUTLINE:

I. Edom—destruction, vv. 1-16

  A. Charge against Edom, vv. 1-9

  B. Crime of Edom, vv. 10-14

  C. Catastrophe to Edom, vv. 15, 16
    (Poetic justice—*lex talionis*—law of retaliation)

II. Israel—restoration, vv. 17-21

  A. Condition of Israel, v. 17

  B. Calling of Israel, v. 18

  C. Consummation of all things, vv. 19-21
    ("And the kingdom shall be the Lord's.")

Jonah

Jonah

Is the book of Jonah the Achilles' heel of the Bible? It is, if we are to accept the ridiculous explanations of the critics. The translators of the Septuagint were the first to question its reasonableness. They set the pattern for the avalanche of criticism that was to follow. The ancient method of modernism is to allegorize the book and to classify it with Robinson Crusoe *and* Gulliver's Travels.

WRITER: Jonah was a historical character. The historical record of the kings of Israel and Judah is accepted as reliable. No one denies that David, Josiah, and Hezekiah were real kings, and it is among the records of these kings that we find the mention of Jonah. Speaking of Jeroboam, the son of Joash, the historian records the name of Jonah (2 Kings 14:25). Jeroboam was a real person; Israel was a real nation; Hamath was a real place. It is unlikely that Jonah, the son of Amittai, was a figment of the imagination.

It is begging the point to say that this is another Jonah. It is not reasonable to believe that there were two Jonahs whose fathers were named Amittai and whose offices were prophets. This is especially evident when it is observed that the name is not a common one (it occurs only in this reference in 2 Kings, in the book of Jonah, and in two references in the New Testament).

Obviously the Lord Jesus Christ considered Jonah a real person, and He accepted the record of the book of Jonah as true (Luke 11:30 and Matthew 12:39-41).

DATE: Conservative scholars place the writing of this book before 745 B.C. The incidents took place about that time. Some even place it as early as 860 B.C. It seems best to place it between 800 and 750 B.C. Students of history will recognize this as the period when Nineveh was in its heyday. The nation of Assyria was at its zenith at this time, also. It was destroyed by 606 B.C. By the time of Herodotus, Nineveh, the city of Nimrod, had ceased to exist. When Xenaphon passed the city it was deserted, but he testified that the walls still stood and they were 150 feet high. Historians now estimate they were at least 100 feet high and 40 feet thick.

COMMENT: Properly speaking, the book of Jonah is not a prophecy and seems to be out of step among the Minor Prophets. It contains no prophecy, although Jonah was a prophet. It is the personal account of a major event in the life of Jonah. As the narrator, he told of his experience, which was a sign of the greatest event in the history of the world—*the resurrection of Jesus Christ.*

There is another salient point to keep before us as we study this book: The fish is not the hero of the story, neither is it the villain. The book is not even about a fish. The chief difficulty is in keeping a correct perspective. The fish is among the props and does not occupy the star's dressing room. Let us distinguish between the essentials and the incidentals. The incidentals are the fish, the gourd, the east wind, the boat, and Nineveh. The essentials are Jehovah and Jonah—God and man.

SIGNIFICANT SUBJECTS:

1 This is the one book of the Old Testament that sets forth the RESURRECTION. Those who assert that the Resurrection is not found in the Old Testament surely are not versed in the magnificent message of Jonah. When a wicked and adulterous generation was seeking after a sign, Jesus referred them to the book of Jonah for the message: "As Jonah … so Jesus" is the fine comparison made by our Lord.

2 SALVATION IS NOT BY WORKS. Salvation is by faith, which leads to repentance. The book of Jonah is read by the Orthodox Jews on the Great Day of Atonement (Yom Kippur). One great self-evident truth from the ritual of this day is that the way to God was not by "works of righteousness which we have done" (Titus 3:5), but by the blood of a substitutionary sacrifice provided by God. The most significant statement in the book of Jonah is in 2:9—"Salvation is of the LORD."

3 GOD'S PURPOSE OF GRACE CANNOT BE FRUSTRATED. If Jonah had refused to go to Nineveh the second time, would God have destroyed the city? God would not have been limited by Jonah's refusal. He would have raised up another instrument, or, more likely, He would have had another fish ready to give Jonah the green light toward Nineveh. The book shows God's determination to get His message of salvation to a people who will hear and accept it.

4 GOD WILL NOT CAST US ASIDE FOR FAITHLESSNESS. When Jonah failed the first time, God did not give him up. The most encouraging words that a faltering and failing child of God can hear are, "And the word of the LORD came unto Jonah the second time" (Jonah 3:1).

5 GOD IS GOOD AND GRACIOUS. The most penetrating picture of God in the entire Bible is in Jonah 4:2. It is wrong to say that the Old Testament reveals a God of wrath and the New Testament reveals a God of love. He is no vengeful deity in the book of Jonah.

6 GOD IS THE GOD OF THE GENTILES. It has been suggested that Romans 3:29 be written over this book: "Is he the God of the Jews only? Is he not also of the Gentiles? Yes, of the Gentiles also." The book of Jonah is the answer to those critics who claim that the Old Testament presents a local and limited deity, a tribal deity. The book of Jonah is a great book on missions and has a world vision.

APPROACHES TO THE STUDY OF JONAH:

1 STRIKING RESEMBLANCE BETWEEN JONAH AND PAUL. Both were missionaries to the Gentiles; both were shipwrecked; both were witnesses to the sailors on board the ship, and both were used to deliver these sailors from death. There are other striking comparisons which a careful study will reveal. Paul made three missionary journeys, and with his trip to Rome, there were four. The four chapters of the book of Jonah may be divided into four missionary journeys of Jonah: (1) into the fish, (2) out onto dry land, (3) to Nineveh, and (4) to the heart of God.

2 TIMETABLE APPROACH. When you consult a timetable in a railroad station or airport, there are three important factors you note: (1) destination, (2) departure time, and (3) arrival time. It is possible to construct the four brief chapters of Jonah into the form of a timetable.

TIMETABLE OF THE BOOK OF JONAH

DEPARTURE	DESTINATION	ARRIVAL	CHAPTER
Israel (Samaria or Gath-hepher)	Nineveh	Fish	1
Fish	Nineveh	Dry land	2
Dry Land	Nineveh	Nineveh	3
Nineveh	Gourd vine	Heart of God	4

Micah

Micah

WRITER: Micah. His name means *Who is like Jehovah?* The word has the same derivation as Michael, which means *Who is like God?* There are many Micahs in Scripture, but this one is identified as a Morasthite (Micah 1:1) since he was an inhabitant of Moresheth-gath (Micah 1:14), a place about 20 miles southwest of Jerusalem, near Lachish. He is not to be confused with any other Micah of Scripture.

TIME: Micah was a contemporary of Isaiah and prophesied during the reigns of Jotham, Ahaz, and Hezekiah (Micah 1:1). He was younger than Isaiah, and his prophecy might be called a miniature Isaiah or Isaiah in shorthand, since there are striking similarities. Ewald and Wellhausen attacked the unity of this book. It is the same attack that has been made against Isaiah.

The ministry of Micah was directed to both Jerusalem and Samaria (Micah 1:1), and he evidently saw the captivity of the Northern Kingdom.

THEME: The judgment and redemption of God, (Micah 7:18). God hates sin, but He loves the souls of the sinners.

STYLE: For many this is the favorite of the Minor Prophets. The writing is pungent and personal. Micah was trenchant, touching, and tender. He was realistic and reportorial—he would have made a good war correspondent. There is an exquisite beauty about this brochure, which combines God's infinite tenderness with His judgments. There are several famous passages that are familiar to the average Christian. Through the gloom of impending judgment, Micah saw clearly the coming glory of the redemption of Israel.

STRIKING STATEMENTS:

Micah 1:6-16	Assyria destroyed Samaria, a miniature of the great destruction of the last days (Micah 4:11-13).
Micah 2:12	The future regathering of the remnant.
Micah 3:6, 7	The end of prophecy.
Micah 3:12; 4:9, 10	Coming destruction of Jerusalem by Babylon and not by Assyria. Jeremiah's life was preserved because of Micah 3:12 (cf. Jeremiah 26:18).
Micah 4:1-8	The coming kingdom over the entire earth (one world).
Micah 5:2	The birth of Christ (quoted in Matthew 2:5, 6).
Micah 5:7, 8	The future ministry of the remnant.
Micah 6:6-8	"One of the most sublime and impassioned declarations of spiritual religion that the Old Testament contains" (Dean Stanley).
Micah 7:18, 19	Micah lived up to his name in exalting God. Dr. Pierson calls it, "A little poem of 12 lines in the Hebrew .... One of the most exquisite things to be found in the entire Old Testament."

COMMENT: Micah pronounced judgment on the cities of Israel and on Jerusalem in Judah. These centers influenced the people of the nation. Micah condemns urban problems that sound very much like our present-day problems: violence, corruption, robbery, covetousness, gross materialism, and spiritual bankruptcy. He could well be labeled "the prophet of the city."

OUTLINE:

The more natural division of the prophecy is to note that Micah gave three messages, each beginning with the injunction, "Hear" (1:2, 3:1, 6:1).

The first was addressed to "all people"; the second was addressed specifically to the leaders of Israel; the third was a personal word of pleading to Israel to repent and return to God.

"WHO IS A GOD LIKE UNTO THEE" IN:

I.   **Proclaiming future judgment for past sins,** Chapters 1–3

    A. Prophet's first message, directed against Samaria, reaches to Jerusalem, Chapter 1

    B. Prophet's second message describes specific sins, Chapter 2

    C. Prophet's third message denounces leaders for sins, Chapter 3

II.   **Prophesying future glory because of past promises,** Chapters 4, 5

    A. Prophecies of last days, Chapter 4

    B. Prophecy of first coming of Christ before second coming and kingdom, Chapter 5

III. **Pleading present repentance because of past redemption,** Chapter 6

IV.   **Pardoning all iniquity because of who God is and what He does,** Chapter 7

Nahum

Nahum

WRITER: Nahum. "Nahum" means *comforter*. He is identified (Nahum 1:1) as an Elkoshite. This is all that is known of the writer of this book. Elkosh was a city in Assyria, a few miles north of the ruins of Nineveh. Nahum could well have lived there and have prophesied to Nineveh, as Daniel did to Babylon later on. The most likely explanation, however, is that there was a village by this name in Galilee. Jerome recorded that a guide pointed out to him such a village as the birthplace of Nahum—but this was a millennium after Nahum lived. Dr. John D. Davis gives the meaning for "Capernaum" as *the village of Nahum*. If "Capernaum" is a Hebrew word, then this is the evident origin.

TIME: There are many dates assigned to this book and this prophet. Dates are given anywhere from 720 to 636 B.C. by conservative scholars. It seems reasonable to locate him about 100 years after Jonah and about 100 years before the destruction of Nineveh— between 660 and 612 B.C. He probably lived during the reign of Hezekiah and saw the destruction of the Northern Kingdom.

THEME: The burden (judgment) of Nineveh (Nahum 1:1).

MESSAGE: Nahum sounds the death-knell of Nineveh and pronounces judgment, by total destruction, on Assyria. God was just in doing this. Jonah, almost a century before, had brought a message from God, and Nineveh had repented. However, the repentance was transitory, and God patiently gave this new generation opportunity to repent (Nahum 1:3). The day of grace ends, and the moment of doom comes (Nahum 3:19). Assyria had served God's purpose (Isaiah 10:5) and would be destroyed. The destruction of Nineveh, according to the details that are given in this written prophecy, is almost breathtaking.

This is a message of comfort to a people who live in fear of a powerful and godless nation. God will destroy any godless nation. Some folk think *Nahum* should be called *Ho-hum!* However, Nahum is a thrilling book to study. It reveals the other side of the attributes of God. God is love, but God is holy and righteous and good.

OUTLINE:

I. **Justice and goodness of God,** Chapter 1:1-8

II. **Justice and goodness of God demonstrated in decision to destroy Nineveh and to give the gospel,** Chapter 1:9-15

III. **Justice and goodness of God exhibited in execution of His decision to destroy Nineveh,** Chapters 2, 3

   A. Annihilation of Assyria, Chapter 2

   B. Avenging action of God justified, Chapter 3

Habakkuk

Habakkuk

WRITER: Habakkuk. His name means *love's embrace*. Martin Luther gave a striking definition of his name, which cannot be improved upon: "Habakkuk signifies an embracer, or one who embraces another, takes him into his arms. He embraces his people and takes them to his arms, i.e., he comforts them and holds them up, as one embraces a weeping child, to quiet it with the assurance that, if God wills, it shall soon be better."

This is all that is known of the writer, except that he was the doubting Thomas of the Old Testament. He had a question mark for a brain.

TIME: Probably written during the reign of Josiah, about the time of the destruction of Nineveh and the rise of Babylon to power. Habakkuk appeared in the twilight, just before the darkness of the captivity.

FORM: The closing statement, "For the chief musician on my stringed instrument" (ARV), reveals that this is a song. The last chapter is a psalm. The entire prophecy is a gem of beauty. It has been translated into a metric version by Dr. Gaebelein. Delitzsch wrote, "His language is classical throughout, full of rare and select turns and words." Moorehouse wrote, "It is distinguished for its magnificent poetry."

MESSAGE: The book opens in gloom and closes in glory. It begins with an interrogation mark and closes with an exclamation point. Habakkuk is a big WHY? Why God permits evil is a question that every thoughtful mind has faced. The book is the answer to the question: Will God straighten out the injustice of the world? This book answers the question: Is God doing anything about the wrongs of the world? This book says that He is. The book is the personal experience of the prophet told in poetry, as Jonah's was told in prose.

THEME: Faith. Habakkuk has been called "the prophet of faith." The great statement of Habakkuk 2:4, "The just shall live by faith," has been quoted three times in the New Testament: Romans 1:17; Galatians 3:11; Hebrews 10:38.

OUTLINE:

I. Perplexity of the prophet, Chapter 1

A. First problem of the prophet, vv. 1-4
Why does God permit evil?

B. God's answer, vv. 5-11
God was raising up Chaldeans to punish Judah (v. 6).

C. Second problem of the prophet (greater than first), vv. 12-17
Why would God permit His people to be punished by a nation more wicked than they? Why did He not destroy the Chaldeans?

II. Perspicuity of the prophet, Chapter 2

A. Practice of the prophet, v. 1
He took the secret problem to the secret place.

B. Patience of the prophet, vv. 2, 3
He waited for the vision.

C. Pageant for the prophet, v. 4
The great divide in humanity: One group, which is crooked, is flowing toward destruction; the other group, by faith, is moving toward God. This is inevitable.

D. Parable to the prophet, vv. 5-20
The application is self-evident from the vision. The Chaldeans, in turn, would be destroyed. God was moving among the nations.

III. Pleasure of the prophet, Chapter 3

A. Prayer of the prophet, vv. 1, 2
The prophet, who thought God was doing nothing about evil, now asks Him to remember to be merciful. Was he afraid that God was doing too much?

B. Program of God, vv. 3-15
God rides majestically in His own chariot of salvation (v. 8).

C. Position of the prophet, vv. 16-19
He will rejoice (v. 18). He has come from pain to pleasure.

Zephaniah

Zephaniah

WRITER: Zephaniah identified himself better than any of the other minor prophets. As Habakkuk concealed himself in silence, Zephaniah went to the opposite extreme more than is ordinary. He traced his lineage back to his great-great-grandfather, who was Hizkiah, whom we know as Hezekiah, king of Judah. Zephaniah was of the royal line (Zephaniah 1:1).

TIME: He located the time of his writing just as clearly as he did his identification—"In the days of Josiah, the son of Amon, king of Judah" (Zephaniah 1:1). According to the arrangement of the Hebrew Scriptures, Zephaniah was the last of the prophets before the captivity. He was contemporary with Jeremiah and probably with Micah. His was the swan song of the Davidic kingdom. He is credited with giving impetus to the revival during the reign of Josiah.

THEME: The dark side of love. Sweetness and light are associated with love on every level, and rightly so, but this aspect does not exhaust the full import of love. Love expresses itself always for the good of the one who is loved. This is the reason that it is difficult to associate love with the judgment of God. The popular notion of God is that He is a super Dr. Jekyll and Mr. Hyde. One nature of His is expressed by love, and the other nature is expressed in wrath by judgment. These two attributes appear to contradict one another to the extent that they seem to be describing two different gods. Zephaniah is filled with the wrath and judgment of God (Zephaniah 1:15; 3:8), but there is the undertone of the love of God (Zephaniah 3:17). It is love that prompts a parent to take the child out of the home to a hospital and to deliver him to the surgeon who endangers the life by pressing a scalpel into the vitals. This act is as much an expression of love as are the candies that are brought to the bedside the next week.

TWO THOUGHTS: Two thoughts stand out in this brief book:

1 "The day of the LORD" occurs seven times. Obadiah and Joel, the first of the writing prophets, were the first to use this expression; Zephaniah, the last, brings it to our attention again. This has particular application to the Great Tribulation, which precedes the kingdom and is included in the day of the Lord. It is a time of wrath.

2 "Jealousy" occurs twice. It is not on the same level as human jealousy, but reveals the love of God for His people who have failed.

OUTLINE:

I. **Judgment of Judah and Jerusalem,** Chapter 1

II. **Judgment of the earth and of all nations,** Chapters 2:1–3:8

III. **Judgments removed; kingdom established,** Chapter 3:9-20

Haggai

Haggai

Prophets to the returned remnant were Haggai, Zechariah, and Malachi.

WRITER: Haggai is mentioned in Ezra 5:1, 2 and 6:14 as one of the two prophets who encouraged the remnant (that returned after the Babylonian captivity) to rebuild the temple in spite of the difficulties that beset them on every hand. From this and the brief references that he made to himself in his prophecy, four things become apparent: (1) he was self-effacing—he exalted the Lord; (2) he was God's messenger—"Thus saith the Lord"; (3) he not only rebuked, he cheered and encouraged; (4) he not only preached, he practiced.

TIME: 520 B.C. "The second year of Darius" enables the historian to pinpoint the time of this prophet in profane history. Hystaspis (Darius mentioned here) began to reign in 521 B.C. At this same time in China, Confucius was living.

THEME: The temple. The reconstruction and refurbishing of the temple were the supreme passion of this prophet. He not only rebuked the people for their delay in rebuilding the temple, but he encouraged them and helped them in this enterprise.

MESSAGE: Haggai constantly referred to the "word of the LORD" as the supreme authority. He willingly humbled himself that the Lord might be exalted. His message was practical. It was as simple and factual as 2 + 2 = 4. The prophecy of Haggai and the epistle of James have much in common. Both put the emphasis upon the daily grind. Action is spiritual; a "do nothing" attitude is wicked. Both placed this yardstick down upon life. Work is the measure of life.

Haggai's contemporary, Zechariah, was visionary and had his head in the clouds, but pragmatic Haggai had both feet on the ground. The man of action and the dreamer need to walk together. First Corinthians 15:58 can appropriately be written over this book.

For the background of his message, read Ezra 3:8-13, also chapters 4 through 6.

KEY VERSES: Haggai 1:8, 14

THE CALENDAR: The compass of this book is three months and 24 days, according to the calendar. There are five messages in the book, and each was given on a specific date. The calendar furnishes the clue for the contents.

OUTLINE:

I. **A challenge to the people,** Chapter 1:1-11
    September 1,520 B.C.

    A. A charge of conflict of interest, vv. 1-4

    B. A call to consider their ways, vv. 5-7

    C. A command to construct the temple, vv. 8-11

II. **The response to the challenge,** Chapter 1:12-15
    September 24, 520 B.C.

    A. Construction of the temple; people obeyed, v. 12

    B. Confirmation from God, vv. 13-15

III. **The discouragement of the people; the encouragement of the Lord,**
    Chapter 2:1-9
    October 21, 520 B.C.
    (The inferiority of the second temple to the first temple became a cause of discouragement, but God responded.)

IV. **An appeal to the Law; the explanation of the principle,** Chapter 2:10-19
    December 24, 520 B.C.

V. **A revelation of God's program; an expectation for the future,** Chapter 2:20-23
    December 24, 520 B.C.

Zechariah

Zechariah

WRITER: Zechariah, whose name means *whom Jehovah remembers*, is identified (1:1) as the son of Berechiah, which means *Jehovah blesses*, and his father was the son of Iddo, which means *the appointed time*. Certainly this cluster of names with such rich meanings is suggestive of the encouragement given to the remnant—God remembers and blesses in the appointed time. The Jewish Targum states that Zechariah was slain in the sanctuary and that this Zechariah was both prophet and priest. In Nehemiah 12:4 Iddo is mentioned as one of the heads of a priestly family. Josephus states that Zechariah, the son of Baruchus, was slain at the temple. There are those who identify Zechariah as the one mentioned by our Lord as having been martyred (Matthew 23:35).

DATE: About 520 B.C. Zechariah was contemporary with Haggai (Ezra 5:1, 6:14), although he was younger (Zechariah 2:4).

CHARACTERISTICS: This book has the characteristics of an apocalypse. The visions resemble those in the books of Daniel and Revelation. Daniel was born in the land of Israel but wrote his apocalypse outside of it. Zechariah was born outside of the land but wrote his within the land. Daniel, Ezekiel, and John all wrote outside the land. Only Zechariah was in Israel when he wrote his apocalypse. In the dark day of discouragement which blanketed the remnant, he saw the glory in all of the rapture and vision of hope. He has more messianic prophecies than any of the other minor prophets.

OUTLINE:

I. **APOCALYPTIC VISIONS (messianic and millennial),** Chapters 1–6

A. Introduction and message of warning, Chapter 1:1-6

B. Ten visions (all in one night), Chapters 1:7–6:15

   1. Riders under myrtle trees, 1:7-17

   2. Four horns, 1:18, 19

   3. Four smiths, 1:20, 21

   4. Man with measuring line, 2

   5. Joshua and Satan, 3:1-7

   6. The Branch, 3:8-10

   7. Lampstand and two olive trees, 4

   8. Flying scroll, 5:1-4

   9. Woman in the ephah, 5:5-11

   10. Four chariots, 6

II. **HISTORIC INTERLUDE,** Chapters 7, 8

A. Question concerning a religious ritual (fasting), Chapter 7:1-3

B. Threefold answer, Chapters 7:4–8:23

   1. When the heart is right, the ritual is right, 7:4-7

   2. When the heart is wrong, the ritual is wrong, 7:8-14

   3. God's purpose concerning Jerusalem unchanged by any ritual, 8

III. **PROPHETIC BURDENS,** Chapters 9–14

A. First burden: Prophetic aspects connected with first coming of Christ, Chapters 9–11

B. Second burden: Prophetic aspects connected with second coming of Christ, Chapters 12–14

Malachi

Malachi

WRITER: "Malachi" means *my messenger*. The Septuagint gives its meaning as *angel*. An angel was a messenger and could be either human or spiritual. There are some who conclude, therefore, that Malachi is only a title and that the name of this prophet is not known. Surely our information of him is as limited as it is regarding the angels. Others have suggested that he was a spiritual angel, but there are no grounds for this.

The message, not the messenger, is the important issue. The Western Union boy is not as important to you as the message he delivers. You want his message, not his or to visit with him.

TIME: Probably 397 B.C. He concluded the prophets, as Nehemiah concluded the historians. He prophesied either during the latter period of Nehemiah's governorship or immediately after it.

MESSAGE: This one, who was the messenger of the Lord, delighted in using his own name when referring to other messengers. He made three mighty references:

1 He referred to Levi as "the messenger of the LORD of hosts" (2:7). This suggests that every witness of God is an *angel* of the Lord.

2 He announced the coming of John the Baptist as "my messenger" (3:1). John the Baptist was the Malachi of the New Testament and began where Malachi of the Old Testament left off. Malachi was the first radio announcer who said, "The next voice you hear will be that of the Lord's messenger."

3 He also made the definite reference to Christ as "the messenger of the covenant" (3:1). The angel of the Lord of the Old Testament is the preincarnate Christ.

The method adopted by Malachi is first to quote a declaration or interrogation God makes to Israel. Then he gives Israel's answer, which is supercilious and sophisticated sarcasm. Finally, he gives God's telling reply, which is equally biting sarcasm.

Malachi's prophecy reveals an age deadened to sin. They were drugged to an unconsciousness of sin. They were in a spiritual stupor with no conviction, which is the lowest state of sin. They mouthed surprise that God would find fault. They were peevish and petulant children who affected ignorance. They pretended to know everything but were woefully lacking in a knowledge of essentials.

OUTLINE:

I.   **The love of God for Israel,** Chapter 1:1-5

II. **The priests reproved for profanity,** Chapters 1:6–2:9

III. **The people rebuked for social sins,** Chapter 2:10-17

IV. **The prediction of the two messengers,** Chapter 3:1-6

V.   **The people rebuked for religious sins,** Chapter 3:7-18

VI. **The prediction of the day of the Lord and of the Sun of Righteousness who ushers it in,** Chapter 4

Gospel of Matthew

Gospel of Matthew

Although it is not alleged that the arrangement of the books of the Bible is inspired, it is a historical fact that spiritual and scholarly men supervised the arrangement of the books of the New Testament canon. Therefore, it is no accident that the Gospel of Matthew is first. Even Renan, the French skeptic, said of this Gospel, "... the most important book in Christendom—the most important book that ever has been written." This Gospel stands like a swinging door between the two Testaments. It swings back into the Old Testament and gathers up prophecies fulfilled at the first coming of Christ, and it swings into the New Testament and speaks of the "new creation" of God, "Upon this rock I will build my church" *(Matthew 16:18).*

WRITER: Matthew was a converted publican (Matthew 9:9) who was chosen to write to the Jews concerning their Messiah.

KEY: Matthew presents the program of God. A proper understanding of the phrase "kingdom of heaven" is essential to any interpretation of the Bible. *The kingdom of heaven and the church are not the same.* The Jews of the first century in Palestine had a clearer understanding of the term than the average church member in

Christendom today. They understood the term to be the sum total of all the prophecies of the Old Testament concerning the coming of the King from heaven to set up a kingdom on this earth with heaven's standard. The concept is not new (Daniel 2:44; 7:14, 27).

OUTLINE: "Behold Your King"—Matthew presents the Lord Jesus Christ as the King.

I. **Person of the King,** Chapters 1, 2

II. **Preparation of the King,** Chapters 3:1–4:16

III. **Propaganda of the King,** Chapters 4:17–9:35

IV. **Program of the King,** Chapters 9:36–16:20

V. **Passion of the King,** Chapters 16:21–27:66

VI. **Power of the King,** Chapter 28

There is a movement in Matthew. Learn to think your way through the entire Gospel from the first chapter through the 28th. *You must know Matthew to understand the Bible.* You can no more understand the Bible without understanding the Gospel of Matthew than you can write without an alphabet.

MOVING THROUGH MATTHEW:

CHAPTER

CHAPTER	
1	Genealogy and record of virgin birth of Jesus
2	Visit of wise men; flight to Egypt; return to Nazareth
3	John the Baptist, forerunner of King, announces kingdom and baptizes Jesus, the King
4	Testing of the King in wilderness; begins public ministry at Capernaum; calls disciples
5, 6, 7	Sermon on the Mount 1 – Relationship of subjects of kingdom to self, 5:1-16 2 – Relationship of subjects of kingdom to Law, 5:17-48 3 – Relationship of subjects of kingdom to God, 6 4 – Relationship of children of King to each other, 7
8	Six miracles of King demonstrate His dynamic to enforce ethics of Sermon on the Mount
9	Performs six more miracles; calls Matthew; contends with Pharisees
10	Jesus commissions 12 to preach gospel of the kingdom to nation Israel

11	Quizzed by disciples of John; rejects unrepentant cities; issues new invitation to individuals
12	Conflict and final break of Jesus with religious rulers
13	Mystery parables of kingdom of heaven
14	John the Baptist beheaded; Jesus feeds 5,000; sends disciples into storm at sea; walks on water to them
15	Jesus denounces scribes and Pharisees; heals daughter of Syrophoenician woman and multitudes; feeds 4,000
16	Conflict with Pharisees and Sadducees; confession from disciples, Peter spokesman; Jesus first confronts them with church, His death and resurrection
17	Transfiguration; demon-possessed boy; tax money provided by miracle
18	Little child; lost sheep; conduct in coming church; forgiveness parable
19	God's standard for marriage and divorce; little children blessed; rich young ruler; apostles' position in coming kingdom
20	Parable of laborers in vineyard; Jesus makes fourth and fifth announcements of His approaching death; mother requests places of honor for James and John; Jesus restores sight to two men
21	King offers Himself publicly and finally to nation; cleanses temple; curses fig tree; condemns religious rulers with parables of two sons and householder
22	Parable of marriage feast for king's son; Jesus answers and silences Herodians, Sadducees, Pharisees
23	Jesus warns against and pronounces woes upon scribes and Pharisees; weeps over Jerusalem
24, 25	Olivet Discourse: Jesus answers questions about sign of end of age and sign of His coming; parable of ten virgins; parable of eight talents; judgment of sheep and goat nations
26	Jesus plotted against; anointed by Mary of Bethany; sold by Judas; observes last Passover and first Lord's Supper; agonizes in Gethsemane; arrested and tried by religious rulers; disowned by Peter
27	Trial, death and burial of the King
28	Resurrection of the King; His great commission

Gospel of Mark

Gospel of Mark

WRITER: John Mark—John was his Jewish name, while Mark was his Latin surname (Acts 12:12). This is the first historical reference to him in Scripture. His mother was a wealthy and prominent Christian in the Jerusalem church. He was a nephew of Barnabas (Colossians 4:10). He evidently was the spiritual son of Simon Peter (1 Peter 5:13). The Gospel of Mark has long been considered Peter's Gospel, as Mark evidently got much of the material in the Gospel record from him. In view of the fact that Simon Peter brought him to a saving knowledge of Christ, it is natural to suppose that he had great influence in Mark's life.

Mark joined Paul and Barnabas before the first missionary journey (Acts 13:5), but he turned back at Perga in Pamphylia (Acts13:13). There is neither need to defend John Mark for turning back nor to explain or excuse his conduct. It is obvious that he failed in the eyes of Paul. Paul's refusal to permit him to accompany them on the second missionary journey is witness enough (Acts 15:37, 38). It severed the combination of Paul and Barnabas (Acts 15:39). Let us hasten to assure you that John Mark made good later on—even Paul acknowledged him as a profitable servant of the Lord (2 Timothy 4:11; also note another reference made by Paul to Mark in Philemon 24).

DATE: Since this was the earliest of the Gospels written, the date of its writing was probably prior to A.D. 63. It is quite likely that it was written from Rome to the Romans. No doubt Mark was with Paul in Rome at the time. The Epistle of Paul to the Romans had preceded him and was in circulation there, so Mark had access to the epistle. It is well to keep in mind that Mark had the *facts* of his Gospel from Peter and the *explanation* of his Gospel from Paul.

THEME: There are two phrases in the first chapter that set before the reader the theme of this Gospel: 1) "The beginning of the gospel of Jesus Christ"—verse 1, and 2) "Jesus came"— verses 9 and 14

Mark presents the beginning of the gospel. It is not the beginning of Jesus Christ, but the beginning of the gospel.

"JESUS CAME"—Mark roots this phrase in the prophecy of Isaiah and the proclamation of John the Baptist, and not in Bethlehem or in Jerusalem as we find in John's Gospel. He begins with Jesus at His baptism, temptation, and His ministry in Galilee. Mark is the Gospel of miracles. Jesus is presented as the Servant of Jehovah (Isaiah 42:1, 2).

Jesus came, in the winsomeness of His humanity and the fullness of His deity, doing good. This was only the beginning of the gospel. He died and rose again. Then He said to His own, "Go." The gospel was then completed. This is the gospel today.

KEY VERSE: Mark 10:45

PECULIAR CHARACTERISTICS: The style of Mark is brief and blunt, pertinent and pithy, short and sweet. Mark is stripped of excess verbiage and goes right to the point. This is the Gospel of action and accomplishment. Here Jesus is not adorned with words and narrative, but He is stripped and girded for action.

Mark is written in a simple style. It is designed for the masses of the street. It is interesting to note that the connective "and" occurs more than any other word in the Gospel. It occurs 1,331 times. It will reward the reader to thumb through the Gospel and note the chapters and verses where this is true. Modern rhetoric might consider it a breach of good grammar, yet there is no word that conveys action as does this word. "And" always leads to further action.

Mark wrote this Gospel in Rome, evidently for Romans. They were a busy people and believed in power and action. This Gospel was brief enough for a busy man to read and would appeal to the Roman mind. Few Old Testament Scriptures are quoted and Jewish customs are explained, which gives additional proof that it was written for foreigners. Mark was written by a busy man for busy people about a busy Person.

OUTLINE: The Credentials of Christ

I. **John INTRODUCES the Servant, Chapter 1:1-8**
    (Death of John, 6:14-29)

II. **God the Father IDENTIFIES the Servant, Chapter 1:9-11**
    (Transfiguration, 9:1-8)

III. **The temptation INITIATES the Servant, Chapter 1:12, 13**

IV. **Work and words ILLUSTRATE (illumine) the Servant, Chapters 1:14–13:37**

   A. Miracles

   1. Healing (physical)

   a. Peter's wife's mother (fever) and others, 1:29-34

   b. Leper, 1:40-45

   c. Palsied man let down through roof, 2:1-12

   d. Man with withered hand, 3:1-5

   e. Many healed beside Sea of Galilee, 3:6-10

   f. Woman with issue of blood, 5:21-34

   g. Sick at Nazareth, 6:5

   h. Disciples heal, 6:13

   i. Sick in land of Gennesaret, 6:53-56

   j. Deaf and dumb of Decapolis, 7:31-37

   k. Blind man of Bethsaida, 8:22-26

   l. Blind Bartimaeus, 10:46-52

2. Nature (natural)
   a. Stills the storm, 4:35-41
   b. 5000 fed, 6:32-44
   c. Walks on sea, 6:45-52
   d. 4000 fed, 8:1-9
   e. Fig tree cursed, 11:12-14
3. Demons (spiritual)
   a. Man in synagogue, 1:21-27
   b. Many demons in Capernaum, 1:32-34
   c. Demons in Galilee, 1:39
   d. Unclean spirits by Sea of Galilee, 3:11, 12
   e. Scribes charge that He casts out demons by Beelzebub, 3:22-30
   f. Demoniac of Gadara, 5:1-20
   g. Syrophoenician's demon-possessed daughter, 7:24-30
   h. Demon-possessed boy, 9:14-27
4. Raised from dead (supernatural); daughter of Jairus, 5:35-43

B. Parables and teachings
   1. Parables
      a. Fasting with the Bridegroom present, 2:19, 20
      b. New cloth on old garment, 2:21
      c. New wine in old bottles, 2:22
      d. Sower, 4:1-20
      e. Candle and bushel, 4:21-25
      f. Seed growing, 4:26-29
      g. Mustard seed, 4:30-34
      h. Man demanding fruit from vineyard, 12:1-12
      i. Fig tree, 13:28-33
      j. Man on trip, 13:34-37
   2. Miscellaneous teachings
      a. Preaching the gospel of the kingdom, 1:14, 15
      b. Preaching in Galilee, 1:28, 35-39

V.   Death, burial, and resurrection INSURE the Servant, Chapters 14:1–16:20

   A. Plot to put Jesus to death, 14:1, 2

   B. Jesus at supper in Bethany, 14:3-9

   C. Judas bargains to betray Jesus, 14:10, 11

   D. The Passover, 14:12-26

   E. The Garden of Gethsemane, 14:27-42

   F. The arrest of Jesus, 14:43-52

   G. The trial of Jesus, 14:53–15:15

   H. The crucifixion of Jesus, 15:16-41

   I. The burial, 15:42-47

   J. The resurrection, 16:1-20

Gospel of Luke

Gospel of Luke

WRITER: Luke was the "beloved physician" of Colossians 4:14. He used more medical terms than Hippocrates, the father of medicine. The choice of Luke by the Holy Spirit to write the third Gospel reveals that there are no accidental writers of Scripture. There was a supernatural selection of Luke. There were "not many wise" called, but Luke belongs to that category. He and Paul were evidently on a very high intellectual level as well as a spiritual level. This partially explains why they traveled together and obviously became fast friends in the Lord.

Dr. Luke would rank as a scientist of his day. He wrote the best Greek of any of the New Testament writers, including Paul. He was also an accurate historian. According to Sir William Ramsay, Dr. Luke was a careful historian of remarkable ability.

A great deal of tradition surrounds the life of Dr. Luke, which is needless for us to examine in a brief analysis. He writes his Gospel from Mary's viewpoint, which confirms the tradition that he got his information for his Gospel from her. Surely he conferred with her. Also there is every reason to believe that he was a Gentile. Most scholars concur in this position. Paul, in Colossians, distinguishes between those "who are of the circumcision" (Colossians

4:11) and the others who are obviously Gentiles. Luke is in the list of Gentiles (Colossians 4:14). Sir William Ramsay and J. M. Stifler affirm without reservation that Luke was a Gentile.

References to Luke: Colossians 4:14; 2 Timothy 4:11; Philemon 24; also the "we" section of Acts—Acts 16:10-17; 20:6; 21:18; 27:1; 28:16.

THEME: "Behold the Man." Jesus is the *second* man but the *last* Adam (1 Corinthians 15:45, 47). God is making men like Jesus (1 John 3:2), therefore Jesus is the *second* man—for there will be the third and even the millionth. He is the *last* Adam, as there will *not* be another head of the human family. Jesus was "made like his brethren" (Hebrews 2:17) that His brethren might be made like Him.

THE SCIENTIFIC APPROACH: Each Gospel presents Jesus from a different viewpoint. Matthew emphasizes that Jesus was born the Messiah. Mark emphasizes that Jesus was the Servant of Jehovah. Luke stresses the fact that Jesus was the perfect Man. John presents the fact that God became a man, but not from the scientific approach.

Dr. Luke states that he examined Jesus of Nazareth, and his findings are that Jesus is God. He came to the same conclusion as John, but his procedure and technique were different.

SPECIAL FEATURES: Although the Gospel of Luke is one of the synoptic Gospels, it contains many features omitted by Matthew and Mark.

- Dr. Luke gives us the songs of Christmas.
- Dr. Luke has the longest account of the virgin birth of Jesus of any of the Gospels. In the first two chapters he gives us an unabashed record of obstetrics, and a clear and candid statement of the virgin birth is given. All the way from Dr. Luke to Dr. Howard Kelly, gynecologist of Johns Hopkins, there is a mighty affirmation of the virgin birth, which makes the statements of pseudo-theologians seem rather puerile when they unblushingly state that the virgin birth is a biological impossibility.
- Dr. Luke gives us 20 miracles, and six of them are recorded in no other Gospel.
- He likewise gives us 23 parables, and 18 of them are found nowhere else. The parables of the prodigal son and the good Samaritan are peculiar to the third Gospel.

- He also gives us the very human account of the walk to Emmaus of our resurrected Lord. This proves that Jesus was still human after His resurrection. Dr. Luke demonstrates that the resurrection was not of the spirit but of the body. Jesus was "sown a natural body ... raised a spiritual *body*" (1 Corinthians 15:44). A definite human sympathy pervades this Gospel, which reveals the truly human nature of Jesus as well as the big-hearted sympathy of this physician of the first century who knew firsthand a great deal about the suffering of humanity.

OUTLINE:

I. **Birth of the Perfect Man and His family,** Chapters 1–3

A. Announcement of the births of John and Jesus; the birth of John, Chapter 1

1. Purpose of Gospel, vv. 1-4 *(Periodic sentence)*

2. Gabriel appears to Zacharias and announces the birth of John, vv. 5-25

3. Gabriel appears to Mary and announces the virgin birth of Jesus, vv. 26-38

4. Mary visits Elisabeth, vv. 39-56 *(Hail Mary* and *Magnificat)*

5. Birth of John (Zacharias' *Benedictus*), vv. 57-80

B. Birth of Jesus; His reception; His circumcision; His journey to Jerusalem at 12 years of age, Chapter 2

1. Birth of Jesus at Bethlehem in a stable, vv. 1-7

2. Reception of Jesus: angels announce His birth to shepherds; shepherds visit stable, vv. 8-20

3. Circumcision of Jesus and purification of Mary, vv. 21-24

4. Incident in temple concerning Simeon, vv. 25-35 *(Nunc Dimittis,* vv. 29-32)

5. Incident in temple concerning Anna; return to Nazareth, vv. 36-40

6. Visit of Joseph, Mary, and Jesus to Jerusalem when Jesus was 12, vv. 41-52 *(Dr. Luke says He was growing normally in body, mind, and spirit—v. 52)*

C. Ministry of John the Baptist; baptism of Jesus; genealogy of Mary, Chapter 3

    1. Ministry of John, vv. 1-20

    2. Baptism of Jesus, vv. 21, 22 (*Trinity*—v. 22)

    3. Genealogy of Mary, vv. 23-38 (*Mary was also descended from David*, v. 31—see Matthew 1)

II. Testing of the Perfect Man; rejection by His hometown, Chapter 4 ("Tempted like as we are," Hebrews 4:15)

A. Temptation of Jesus, vv. 1-13

B. Jesus returns to Galilee and Nazareth; rejected by His hometown, vv. 14-30 *(Jesus quotes from Isaiah 61:1-2 in v. 18)*

C. Jesus moves His headquarters to Capernaum; continues His ministry, vv. 31-44

III. Ministry of the Perfect Man in area of Galilee, Chapters 5–9

A. Jesus calls disciples for the second time; cleanses lepers; heals man with palsy; calls Matthew; gives parables on new garment and wine skins, Chapter 5

B. Jesus defends disciples for plucking grain on Sabbath; heals paralyzed man on Sabbath; chooses 12; gives Sermon on the Plain, Chapter 6

C. Jesus heals centurion's servant; restores to life son of widow of Nain; commends John the Baptist; goes to dinner at Pharisee's house; gives parable of two debtors, Chapter 7

D. Jesus gives parables: sower, lighted candle, personal relationships; stills storm; casts out demons at Gadara; heals woman with issue of blood; restores to life daughter of Jairus, Chapter 8

E. Jesus commissions and sends forth the Twelve; feeds 5000; announces death and resurrection; transfigured; casts out demons from an only son; sets His face toward Jerusalem; puts down test for discipleship, Chapter 9

IV. Ministry of the Perfect Man on way to Jerusalem, Chapters 10–18

A. Jesus sends forth the 70; pronounces judgment on Chorazin, Bethsaida, and Capernaum; gives parable of Good Samaritan; enters home of Mary and Martha, Chapter 10

B. Jesus teaches disciples to pray by using parables of the persistent friend and a good father; accused of casting out demons by Beelzebub; gives parables—unclean spirit leaving a man, sign of Jonah, lighted candle; denounces Pharisees, Chapter 11

C. Jesus warns of leaven of Pharisees; gives parables of rich fool, return from wedding, testing of servants in light of coming of Christ; states He is a divider of men, Chapter 12

D. Jesus teaches men not to judge but repent; gives parable of fig tree; heals woman with infirmity; gives parables of mustard seed and leaven; continues to teach as He goes toward Jerusalem; weeps over Jerusalem, Chapter 13

E. Jesus goes to dinner at home of Pharisee; gives parables of impolite guests, the great supper, building a tower, king going to war, salt that loses its tang, Chapter 14

F. Jesus gives parable of lost sheep, lost coin, two lost sons (prodigal son), Chapter 15
   (The obedient Son is the One giving the parable.)

G. Jesus gives parable about unjust steward; answers covetous Pharisees; speaks on divorce; recounts incident of rich man and Lazarus (poor man), Chapter 16

H. Jesus instructs His disciples on forgiveness, faithful service; heals ten lepers (one Samaritan returns to give thanks); speaks on spiritual nature of kingdom and His coming again, Chapter 17

I. Jesus gives two parables on prayer; blesses little children; confronts rich young ruler with five of Ten Commandments; heals blind man on entering Jericho, Chapter 18

V.   **Ministry of the Perfect Man in Jericho and Jerusalem,** Chapters 19–21

A. Jesus enters Jericho and home of Zacchaeus; conversion of Zacchaeus; gives parable of ten pounds; enters Jerusalem; weeps over city; cleanses temple, Chapter 19

B. Jesus' authority challenged; gives parable of vineyard; questioned about paying tribute to Caesar; silences Sadducees about resurrection; questions scribes, Chapter 20

C. Jesus notes how people give, commends widow; answers question in Olivet Discourse, "When shall these things be?" Chapter 21

VI.   **Betrayal, trial, and death of the Perfect Man,** Chapters 22, 23
     (Our Kinsman-Redeemer)

A. Judas plots with chief priests to betray Jesus; Jesus plans for last Passover and institutes Lord's Supper; announces His betrayal, position of apostles in future kingdom; Peter's denial; warns disciples of future; goes to Gethsemane; betrayed by Judas; arrested and led to high priest's house; denied by Peter; mocked, beaten, brought before Sanhedrin, Chapter 22

B. Jesus brought before Pilate and Herod; Barabbas released; Jesus foretells destruction of Jerusalem and prays for His enemies; Jesus crucified; mocked by rulers, soldiers, one thief; other thief turns to Jesus and is accepted by Him; dismisses His spirit; placed in new tomb of Joseph of Arimathaea, Chapter 23

VII. Resurrection of the Perfect Man, Chapter 24:1-48

   A. Jesus raised from the dead; leaves Joseph's tomb, vv. 1-12

   B. Jesus goes down road to Emmaus, reveals Himself to two disciples, vv. 13-34

   C. Jesus goes to the assembled disciples, reveals Himself to the 11; gives commission to go, vv. 35-48 *(He is still a man; emphasizes the importance of the Word of God)*

VIII. Ascension of the Perfect Man, Chapter 24:49-53 (Jesus promises to send Holy Spirit; ascends to heaven in attitude of blessing His own)

Gospel of John

Gospel of John

WRITER: John, the apostle, son of Zebedee and Salome, and brother of James (Mark 1:19, 20; Matthew 20:20; John 21:20-24). His authorship has been seriously questioned by the Tubingen school of critics; however, the objections have been fully answered by the Dead Sea scrolls and also by the dating of carbon 14, and the Johannean authorship is received by competent Bible scholarship.

It is interesting to note that the following early church fathers ascribe the fourth Gospel to John: Theophilus, Bishop of Antioch—A.D. 180; Iranaeus—A.D. 190, pupil of Polycarp, who in turn was pupil of John; Clement of Alexandria—A.D. 200; and the Muratorium fragment says the fourth Gospel is by John.

DATE: A.D. 90-100. Some suppose that this is the last book of the New Testament to be written. However, it seems appropriate to consider the writings of John in sequence: namely, the Gospel of John, the three Epistles, and the Revelation. All were written evidently during the last ten years of the life of the "beloved apostle."

STRUCTURE:

There are several striking features about the structure:

1 The first three Gospels are called the Synoptic Gospels because they are written from the same viewpoint. The fourth Gospel is different.

> **A** Matthew and Mark emphasize the miracles of Jesus, and Luke gives attention to the parables; John does neither.

> **B** The miracles in John are given as signs and were chosen with a great deal of discrimination in order to interpret certain great truths (e.g., Jesus fed the 5000, and following it is His discourse on the Bread of Life). There are 11 specific signs in John.

> **C** There are no parables in the fourth Gospel. The word "parable" occurs one time (John 10:6), but is not the regular Greek word *parabole* but *paroimia*. The story of the Good Shepherd is not a parable but a discourse. The record of the lost sheep in Luke 15 is a parable. In John, the figures that Jesus used are in the nature of metaphors.

2 The simplicity of language has caused some to label John's record as the "simple Gospel." The fact that so many monosyllabic and disyllabic words occur has deceived many. This is the most profound Gospel, and the most difficult to fathom its meaning. Consider this simple statement and then try to probe its depths: "... ye in me, and I in you" (John 14:20).

3 John gives a chronological order which is well to note (e.g., "the next day," John 1:29, 35, 43). He presents a logical and chronological sequence of events. He also gives attention to places and cities (e.g., "Bethabara beyond the Jordan," John 1:28; "Cana, of Galilee," John 2:1).

4 Although the deity of Christ is in the foreground, the humanity of Christ is peculiarly emphasized (e.g., "Jesus ... being wearied with his journey," John 4:6).

5 The name *Jesus* is used almost entirely to the exclusion of *Christ*. This seems strange in a Gospel that sets forth His deity.

6 The word *Jew* occurs over 60 times.

WHY JOHN WROTE:

Several explanations have been offered as the reasons why John wrote his Gospel:

1 – To correct Synoptic Gospels (invalid since he did not deal with their material);

2 – To correct a wrong view concerning John the Baptist;

3 – To refute errors of Cerinthus;

4 – John's own reason—John 20:30, 31.

ESTIMATION: During the entire life of the church there have been many glowing tributes paid to the fourth Gospel. Some have called this "the heart of Christ," the "spiritual Gospel," and in Europe it is called "the bosom of Christ."

THEME: The deity of Jesus is the paramount purpose. The Messianic character also holds priority. This is succinctly stated in John 20:31—"But these are written, that ye might believe that Jesus is the Christ, the Son of God; and that believing ye might have life through his name."

There is a mighty movement stated in John 16:28—"I came forth from the Father, and am come into the world: again, I leave the world, and go to the Father." God became a man; this is the simple statement of the sublime fact. John Wesley expressed it, "God contracted to a span."

These things are recorded to beget faith in the heart of man. "Believe" is used over 100 times in John's Gospel. It occurs fewer than 40 times in the Synoptic Gospels. The noun "faith" does not occur in John but is used in the other Gospels. "Eternal life" occurs 35 times in John, but only 12 times in the Synoptic Gospels.

OUTLINE:

I.   Prologue—incarnation, Chapter 1:1-18

A. Word is God, vv. 1-3

B. Word became flesh, v. 14

C. Word revealed God, v. 18

II.   Introduction, Chapter 1:19-51

A. Witness of John the Baptist, vv. 19-36
Jesus is Revealer of God (v. 36); Redeemer of man (v. 29)

B. Witness of Andrew, vv. 37-42
Jesus is the Messiah [Christ] (v. 41)

C. Witness of Philip, vv. 43-46
Jesus is fulfillment of Old Testament (v. 45)

D. Witness of Nathanael, vv. 47-51
Jesus is Son of God, King of Israel (v. 49)

III.   Witness of works and words ("signs" 20:30, 31), Chapters 2–12

A. Jesus at marriage in Cana (first work), Chapter 2:1-12

B. Jesus cleanses temple during Passover in Jerusalem (first word), Chapter 2:13-22
Jesus is Resurrection (v. 22)

C. Jesus interviews Nicodemus in Jerusalem (second word), Chapters 2:23–3:36
Jesus must die for sins of world (3:15)

D. Jesus interviews woman at well in Sychar (third word), Chapter 4:1-45
Jesus is giver of Water of Life

E. Jesus heals nobleman's son in Capernaum (second work), Chapter 4:46-54

F. Jesus heals man at pool of Bethesda (third work), Chapter 5
Jesus is equal with God

G. Jesus feeds 5,000 on east of Sea of Galilee (fourth work & word), Chapter 6
Jesus is Bread of Life

H. Jesus teaches at Feast of Tabernacles in temple (fifth word), Chapter 7
Jesus is Water of Life; promises the Holy Spirit

I. Jesus in temple forgives woman taken in adultery (sixth word), Chapter 8
Jesus is Light of World

3. Trial before high priest, vv. 19-24

4. Second denial by Simon Peter, vv. 25-27

5. Trial before Pilate, vv. 28-40

B. Death of Jesus at Golgotha; burial in tomb of Joseph, Chapter 19

C. Resurrection of Jesus; appearances to Mary, disciples, Thomas, Chapter 20

VI. **Epilogue—glorification,** Chapter 21
    The resurrected Jesus is still God
    Lord of our wills—directs our service (v. 6)
    Lord of our hearts—motive for service (vv. 15-17)
    Lord of our minds—lack of knowledge no excuse from service (v. 22)

Another division of the Gospel of John:

John 1–12	LIGHT
John 13–17	LOVE
John 18–21	LIFE

Acts

Acts

(Sometimes called the fifth Gospel, it is a continuation of the Gospel of Luke)

Last recorded fact about Jesus in the Gospels:

Matthew—Resurrection	
Mark—Ascension	**ACTS 1 BRINGS ALL FOUR TOGETHER.**
Luke—Promise of the Holy Spirit	
John—Promise of the Second Coming	

The great missionary commission given in the four Gospels is confirmed in Acts.

Acts furnishes a ladder on which to place the Epistles.

Acts is a bridge between the Gospels and the Epistles.

The New Testament without Acts leaves a great, yawning gap. "If the book of Acts were gone, there would be nothing to replace it" (Howson).

WRITER: Dr. Luke, who also wrote the third Gospel (Acts 1:1). Sir William Ramsay says that Luke is the greatest of all historians, ancient or modern.

DATE: About A.D. 63. Acts covers a period of approximately 30 years. This is the inspired record of the beginnings of the church. While Genesis records the origin of the physical universe, Acts records the origin of the spiritual body.

KEY VERSE: Acts 1:8

SPECIAL FEATURES:

1 – Prominence of the Lord Jesus Christ.

2 – Prominence of the Holy Spirit. Christ promised to send the Holy Spirit (John 7:37-39; John 14:16, 17; John 20:22; Acts 1:8). This is the age of the Holy Spirit. The great fact of this age is the indwelling of the Holy Spirit (1 Corinthians 6:19).

3 – Power of the church.

4 – Prominence of the church, visible and invisible (a new institution).

5 – Prominence of places—begins in Jerusalem, ends in Rome. (Ramsay checked the many places referred to.)

6 – Prominence of persons—Dr. Luke mentions 110 persons by name.

7 – Prominence of the resurrection, the center of gospel preaching.

8 – Prominence of Peter in the first section, and Paul in the last section. (There is a strange omission of the other apostles.)

OUTLINE:

I.   The Lord Jesus Christ at work by the Holy Spirit through the apostles in Jerusalem, Chapters 1–7

A. Preparation for the coming of the Spirit, Chapter 1

   1. Introduction, vv. 1, 2

   2. 40 days post-resurrection ministry of Jesus, vv. 3-9

   3. Ascension and promise of the return of Jesus, vv. 10, 11

   4. Waiting for the Spirit, vv. 12-14

   5. Appointment of an apostle, vv. 15-26

B. Day of Pentecost (Bethlehem of the Holy Spirit), Chapter 2

   1. Coming of the Holy Spirit, vv. 1-13

   2. First sermon in the church age by Peter, vv. 14-47

C. First miracle of the church; Peter's second sermon, Chapter 3

   1. Healing of lame man, vv. 1-11

   2. Appealing and revealing address of Peter, vv. 12-26

   3. Believing 5000 men (results), 4:4

D. First persecution of the church; power of the Holy Spirit, Chapter 4

E. Death of Ananias and Sapphira; second persecution, Chapter 5
(Discipline within and persecution without)

F. Appointment of deacons; witness of Stephen, a deacon, Chapter 6

G. Stephen's address and martyrdom (first martyr), Chapter 7

II. The Lord Jesus Christ at work by the Holy Spirit through the apostles in Judæa and Samaria, Chapters 8–12

A. Conversion of Ethiopian Eunuch (son of Ham), Chapter 8

B. Conversion of Saul of Tarsus (son of Shem), Chapter 9

C. Conversion of Cornelius, Roman centurion (son of Japheth), Chapter 10

D. Peter defends his ministry; gospel goes to Antioch, Chapter 11

E. Death of James; arrest of Peter, Chapter 12

III. **The Lord Jesus Christ at work by the Holy Spirit through the apostles to the uttermost part of the earth,** Chapters 13–28

A. First missionary journey of Paul, Chapters 13, 14

B. Council at Jerusalem, Chapter 15

C. Second missionary journey of Paul, Chapters 15:36–16:40

D. Second missionary journey (continued)
Paul in Thessalonica, Athens, Chapter 17

E. Second missionary journey (concluded)
Paul in Corinth; Apollos in Ephesus, Chapter 18

F. Third missionary journey, Chapters 18:23–21:14
Paul in Ephesus, Chapter 19

G. Third missionary journey of Paul (continued), Chapter 20

H. Paul goes to Jerusalem and is arrested, Chapter 21

I. Paul's defense before the mob at Jerusalem, Chapter 22

J. Paul's defense before the Sanhedrin, Chapter 23

K. Paul before Felix, Chapter 24

L. Paul before Festus, Chapter 25

M. Paul before Agrippa, Chapter 26

N. Paul goes to Rome via storm and shipwreck, Chapter 27

O. Paul arrives in Rome, Chapter 28
(Last seen preaching to Gentiles)

PAUL'S FIRST MISSIONARY JOURNEY

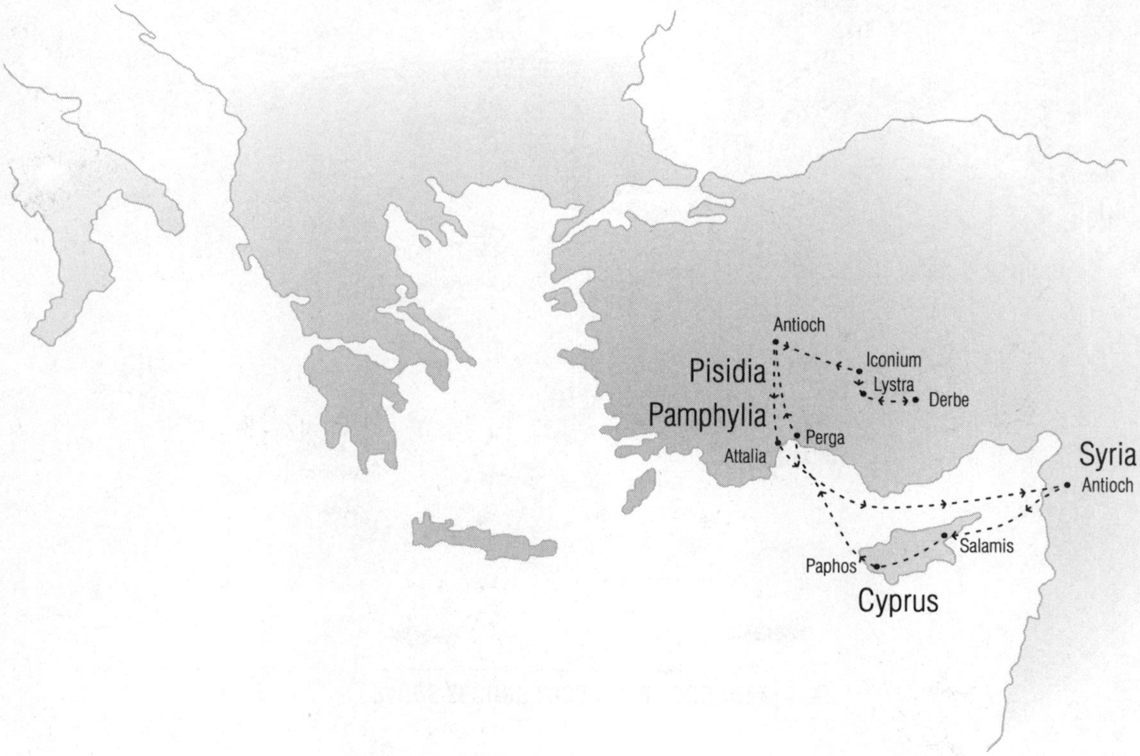

Syria
Antioch

Salamis

Cyprus

Paphos

Iconium
Derbe
Lystra

Antioch

Perga

Pisidia

Pamphylia

Attalia

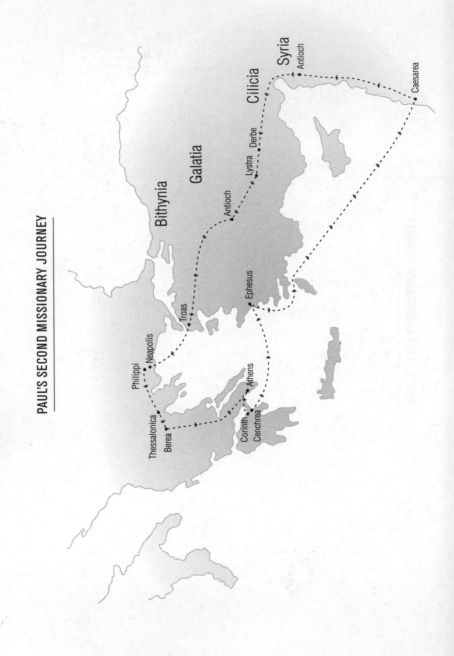

PAUL'S SECOND MISSIONARY JOURNEY

Syria
Antioch
Caesarea
Cilicia
Derbe
Lystra
Galatia
Antioch
Bithynia
Ephesus
Troas
Neapolis
Philippi
Thessalonica
Berea
Athens
Corinth
Cenchrea

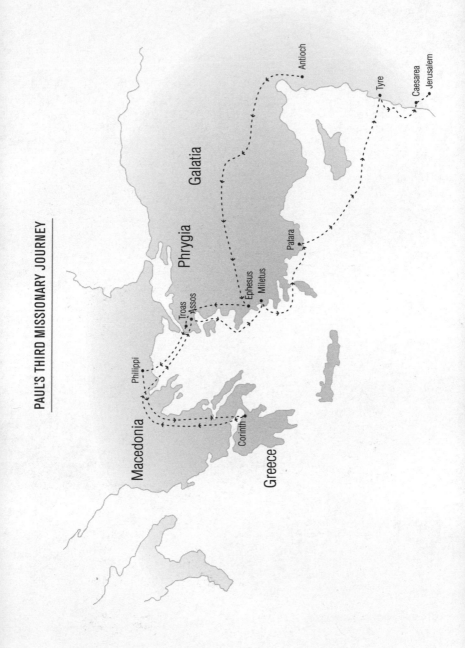

PAUL'S THIRD MISSIONARY JOURNEY

Antioch

Tyre

Caesarea

Jerusalem

Galatia

Phrygia

Patara

Ephesus

Miletus

Troas

Assos

Philippi

Macedonia

Corinth

Greece

Romans

Romans

WRITER: Paul

DATE: A.D. 57-58

PLACE: Corinth. This epistle was written during Paul's third missionary journey, at Corinth where he spent three months (January to March, A.D. 57). He had just come from Ephesus where he had spent three strenuous years.

OCCASION: This letter was brought forth by natural reason. Paul wished to visit Rome on his way to Spain. The letter was taken by Phoebe, deaconess of Cenchrea (Romans 16:1).

SUBJECT: The righteousness of God.

There is a personal note running through all the epistles of Paul, including Romans. Nevertheless, Romans contains the great gospel manifesto for the world. To Paul, the gospel was the great ecumenical movement and Rome was the center of that world for which Christ died. Romans is an eloquent and passionate declaration of the gospel of Jesus Christ by a man who made an arduous but productive journey to die for Christ, the One who died for him. Romans is more than cold logic; it is the gospel stated in warm love.

KEY VERSES: Romans 1:16, 17

ESTIMATION: The reading of Romans is one of the most rewarding experiences in the life of a Christian. This is not to say that it should be read as a magazine article that is put aside and dismissed from the mind. The continual reading of this epistle brings a stream of benefits to the believer. The investment of a great amount of time pays handsome dividends on the spiritual market.

Romans requires all the mental make-up we have, and then it must be bathed in prayer and supplication before the Holy Spirit can teach us.

This epistle *is* the greatest document on our salvation! William Newell says that Romans is the gospel. Every Christian should make an effort to know Romans, for this book will ground the believer in the faith.

READ ROMANS REGULARLY–REALLY READ ROMANS

These three features will become dominant in the life of one who constantly reads Romans:

UNDERSTANDING of the basic facts of salvation

UNUSUAL CONVICTION about matters pertaining to the faith

USEFULNESS in practical Christian service

OUTLINE (in brief):

1 – Salutation 1:1-17	7 – Security 8:28-39
2 – Sin 1:18–3:20	8 – Segregation 9–11
3 – Salvation 3:21–5:11	9 – Sacrifice & service 12, 13
4 – Sanctification 5:12–6:23	10 – Separation 14, 15
5 – Struggle 7	11 – Salutation 16
6 – Spirit-filled living 8:1-27	

OUTLINE:

I. Doctrinal, "Faith," Chapters 1—8

A. Justification of the sinner, Chapters 1:1—5:11

    1. Introduction, 1:1-17

      a. Paul's personal greeting, 1:1-7

      b. Paul's personal purpose, 1:8-13

      c. Paul's three "I am's," 1:14-17
        Key verses 16, 17—the revelation of the righteousness of God.

    2. Revelation of the sin of man, 1:18—3:20
      This is "Sinnerama." Universal fact: Man is a sinner.
      Ecumenical movement is away from God. Axiom: World is
      guilty before God—all need righteousness.

      a. Revelation of the wrath of God against sin of man, 1:18-32

        i. Natural revelation of God (original version), vv. 18-20

        ii. Sub-natural response of man (reversion), vv. 21-23

        iii. Unnatural retrogression of man (perversion), vv. 4-27

        iv. Supernatural requital of God (inversion), vv. 28-32

      b. Revelation of the sin of good people, 2:1-16
        Respectable people need righteousness.

      c. Revelation of the sin of Israel under the Law, 2:17—3:8

      d. Revelation of the universality of sin, 3:9-20

        i. Judge's verdict of guilty against mankind, vv. 9-12
          Man cannot remove guilt.

        ii. Great Physician's diagnosis of mankind, vv. 13-18
          Man cannot change his nature. Man has an incurable disease.

        iii. Purpose of the Law, vv. 19, 20
          Law reveals sin, not salvation. Last word is "sin" (v. 20).

    3. Revelation of the righteousness of God, 3:21—5:11
    Righteousness provided.
    Righteousness of God defined—not the character of God
    nor self-righteousness of man.

a. Justification by faith explained, 3:21-31

DEFINITION: Justification is the act of God that declares a sinner righteous by faith on the merit of Christ's sacrifice. It is the addition of the righteousness of Christ as well as the subtraction of sins.

- *Propitiation—"mercy seat" (Hebrews 9:5)*
- *Redemption—to pay a price for deliverance*
- *Propitiation is toward God.*
- *Redemption is toward sin.*

b. Justification by faith *illustrated*, 4:1-25
(Demonstration—Abraham and David)

c. Justification by faith—*results derived*, 5:1-11
Eight benefits:

   i. Peace, v. 1

   ii. Access, v. 2

   iii. Hope, v. 2

   iv. Patience—fruit of tribulations, v. 3

   v. Love, v. 5

   vi. Holy Spirit, v. 5

   vii. Deliverance from the Great Tribulation, v. 9

   viii. Joy, v. 11

Reconciliation is toward man. Definition: Change from enmity to friendship. Justification by faith is an act of God which is permanent.

B. Sanctification of the saint, Chapters 5:12–8:39

1. Potential sanctification, 5:12-21
Federal headship of Adam and Christ

a. Headship of Adam, vv. 12-14
Death—sin

b. Headship of Christ, vv. 15-17
Life—righteousness

c. Offense of Adam vs. righteousness of Christ, vv. 18-21

- Disobedience vs. Obedience
- Judgment vs. Free Gift
- Sin vs. Grace
- Condemnation vs. Justification

2. Positional sanctification, 6:1-10
   Union with Christ in His death and resurrection is the basis of deliverance from sin.

3. Practical sanctification, 6:11-23
   Obedience to God leads to the experience of deliverance from sin.

4. Powerless sanctification, 7:1-25

   a. **Shackles of a saved soul,** vv. 1-14
      Spiritual emancipation

   b. **Struggle of a saved soul,** vv. 15-25
      Civil war (No good in old nature, no power in new nature)

5. God's new provision for sanctification, 8:1-39
   (Powerful sanctification)

   a. **New law: Holy Spirit vs. Law,** vv. 1-4

   b. **New struggle: Holy Spirit vs. flesh,** vv. 5-13

   c. **New man, son of God: Holy Spirit and spirit of man,** vv. 14-17

   d. **New creation: old vs. new, bondage vs. liberty,** vv. 18-22

   e. **New body: groaning vs. redeemed body,** vv. 23-27
      Holy Spirit helps us in our present bodies.

   f. **New purpose of God,** vv. 28-34
      God's purpose guarantees the salvation of sinners.

   g. **New security of the believer,** vv. 35-39
      God's love guarantees the security of the believer.

II. **Dispensational, "Hope,"** Chapters 9–11

   A. **God's past dealings with Israel,** Chapter 9

      1. Israel defined, vv. 1-5

      2. Israel identified, vv. 6-13

      3. Choice of Israel in the sovereign purpose of God, vv. 14-24

      4. Choice of Gentiles in the scriptural prophecies of God, vv. 25-33

   B. **God's present purpose with Israel,** Chapter 10

      1. Present state of Israel—lost, vv. 1-4
         Reason: Christ is the end of the law for righteousness.

      2. Present standing of Israel—same as Gentiles, vv. 5-12
         "For there is no difference."

3. Present salvation for both Jew and Gentile—hear and believe the gospel, vv. 13-21

C. God's future purpose with Israel, Chapter 11
Remnant regathered as a nation and redeemed.

1. Remnant of Israel finding salvation, vv. 1-6

2. Remainder of Israel blinded, vv. 7-12

3. Reason for setting aside the nation Israel—salvation of the Gentiles, vv. 13-21

4. Restoration of nation Israel—greater blessing, vv. 22-32

5. Reason for restoring the nation Israel, vv. 33-36
Locked in the riches of the wisdom of God.

III. Duty, "Love," Chapters 12–16

A. Service of "the sons of God," Chapters 12, 13

1. Relationship to God ("present—yield"), 12:1-2

2. Relationship to gifts of the Spirit, 12:3-8

3. Relationship to other believers, 12:9-16

4. Relationship to unbelievers, 12:17-21

5. Relationship to government, 13:1-7

6. Relationship to neighbors, 13:8-14

B. Separation of "the sons of God," Chapters 14–16

1. Relationship to weak believers, 14:1—15:3
   Three principles of conduct for Christians

   a. Conviction, 14:5

   b. Conscience, 14:22

   c. Consideration, 15:1-3

2. Relationship of Jews and Gentiles as believers, 15:4-13 (Racial relationships)

3. Relationship of Paul to Romans and Gentiles generally, 15:14-33 (The gospel and Gentiles, v. 16)

4. Relationship of Christians to one another demonstrated, 16:1-27
   35 individuals mentioned by name—mutual love and tender affection.

1 & 2 Corinthians

1 & 2 Corinthians

WRITER: Paul

DATE: A.D. 55-57 (more likely 57)

PLACE: Ephesus

SUBJECT: The Lordship of Jesus (1 Corinthians 1:2, 3, 7-10)

BACKGROUND: Carnal Corinth was the sin center of the Roman Empire in Paul's day. It was labeled "Vanity Fair." Its location was about 40 miles west of Athens on a narrow isthmus between Peloponnesus and the mainland. It was the great commercial center of the Roman Empire with three harbors, of which two were important—Lechaeum, about one and a half miles to the west, and Cenchreae, about eight and a half miles to the east.

196 B.C.	Rome declared it a free city.
146 B.C.	It rebelled and was totally destroyed by Mummius, the consul.
46 B.C.	Julius Caesar rebuilt the city in great elegance, restoring it to its former prominence.

However, even its ruins were lost to history for many years, and a fishing village was built over them. In 1928, an earthquake uncovered them, and now much of the city has been excavated.

The temple of Aphrodite, built on the Acrocorinthus, was attended by 1,000 priestesses of vice, actually nothing more than prostitutes. The city was given over to licentiousness and pleasure. The Isthmian games were conducted here.

Against this corrupt background, Paul preached the gospel in Corinth, founded the church, and wrote two epistles to the church at Corinth: 1 and 2 Corinthians. (Read Acts 18:1-18 for the account of Paul's visit to Corinth.)

1 CORINTHIANS

COMMENT: First Corinthians is obviously Paul's answer to a previous letter that he had written to the Corinthians (1 Corinthians 5:9). They sent a delegation with a letter (1 Corinthians 7:1; 16:17) and 1 Corinthians is Paul's reply concerning the conditions in the Corinthian church. It is a letter of correction of errors and confirmation of truth.

OUTLINE:

I.   **Salutation and thanksgiving,** Chapter 1:1-9

II. **Concerning conditions in the Corinthian church,** Chapters 1:10–16:9

A. Concerning DIVISIONS and party spirit, Chapters 1:10–4:21

1. Centrality of Christ crucified
Corrects divisions, 1:10-31

2. Clarity of Holy Spirit
Corrects human wisdom, 2

3. Correct conception of God
Clarifies Christian service, 3

4. Conditions of Christ's servants
Constrain Christian conduct, 4

B. Concerning SCANDALS in the Corinthian church, Chapters 5, 6

1. Impurity, 5

2. Lawsuits among members, 6

C. Concerning MARRIAGE, Chapter 7

D. Concerning CHRISTIAN LIBERTY, Chapters 8:1 –11:1

   1. Liberty of the minister, 9

   2. Liberty is not license, 10:1—11:1

E. Concerning WOMAN'S DRESS, Chapter 11:2-16

F. Concerning the LORD'S TABLE, Chapter 11:17-34

G. Concerning SPIRITUAL GIFTS, Chapters 12–14

   1. Endowment of gifts, 12

     a. Gifts are given to maintain unity in diversity, vv. 1-11

     b. Members of human body compared to gifts of Holy Spirit, vv. 12-31

   2. Energy of gifts—Love, 13

   3. Exercise of gifts, 14

     a. Gift of prophecy is superior to gift of tongues, vv. 1-22

     b. Order in local church for exercise of any gift, vv. 23-40

H. Concerning the GOSPEL, Chapter 15

   1. Prominence of resurrection in the gospel, vv. 1-4

   2. Proofs of resurrection, vv. 5-19

   3. Parade of resurrection, vv. 20-28

     a. Christ, the firstfruits

     b. Those who are Christ's (the church)

     c. Old Testament saints, Tribulation saints

     d. Kingdom set up, Christ reigning

     e. Death destroyed

     f. Christ returns to His place in the Trinity

   4. Program and pattern of resurrection, vv. 29-50

   5. Power of resurrection, vv. 51-58

I. Concerning COLLECTIONS, Chapter 16:1-9

III.   Closing exhortations and benediction, Chapter 16:10-24

2 CORINTHIANS

COMMENT: Shortly after Paul had written 1 Corinthians from Ephesus, where he was in grave danger (2 Corinthians 1:8), he wrote 2 Corinthians from Philippi. Paul was in Ephesus approximately three years. He had sent Titus to Corinth because he could not personally go there at that time. Timothy was with Paul in Ephesus, and these two proceeded to Troas to wait for Titus to bring word from Corinth (2 Corinthians 2:12, 13). When Titus did not come, Paul and Timothy went on to Philippi where Titus brought good news from Corinth (2 Corinthians 7:5-11). Any breach between Paul and the Corinthian church was healed.

This epistle is difficult to outline, as it is less organized than any of Paul's other letters—but it contains more personal details. In each chapter there is always a minor theme developed (which sometimes seems to take the place of the major theme) and generally expressed in some striking verse. This may explain the seeming difficulty in outlining and organizing this epistle. We will note this as we consider each chapter.

First Corinthians deals with conditions and *corrections* in the church. Second Corinthians deals with conditions of the *ministry* within the church.

OUTLINE:

I. **COMFORT of God,** Chapters 1–7
   (Christian living)

   A. Introduction, Chapter 1:1, 2

   B. God's comfort for life's plans, Chapter 1:3-24

   C. God's comfort in restoring a sinning saint, Chapter 2

   D. God's comfort in the glorious ministry of Christ, Chapter 3

   E. God's comfort in the ministry of suffering for Christ, Chapter 4

   F. God's comfort in the ministry of martyrdom for Christ, Chapter 5

   G. God's comfort in all circumstances of the ministry of Christ, Chapter 6

   H. God's comfort in the heart of Paul, Chapter 7

II. **COLLECTION for poor saints at Jerusalem,** Chapters 8, 9
   (Christian giving)

   A. Example of Christian giving, Chapter 8:1-6

   B. Exhortation to Christian giving, Chapter 8:7-15

   C. Explanation of Christian giving, Chapters 8:16–9:5

   D. Encouragement to Christian giving, Chapter 9:6-15

III. **CALLING of the apostle Paul,** Chapters 10–13
   (Christian guarding)

   A. Authentication of Paul's apostleship, Chapter 10

   B. Vindication of Paul's apostleship, Chapter 11

   C. Revelation of Paul's apostleship, Chapter 12

   D. Execution of Paul's apostleship, Chapter 13:1-10

   E. Conclusion of Paul's apostleship, Chapter 13:11-14

Galatians

Galatians

WRITER: Paul (Galatians 1:1)

DATE: About A.D. 57. This epistle was probably written on the third missionary journey from Ephesus, during Paul's two years of residence there. There is substantial basis, however, for the claim that it was written from Corinth, shortly before Paul wrote the Epistle to the Romans. Dr. Lenski advances the theory that it was written from Corinth on the second missionary journey, about April, A.D. 53.

OCCASION: Paul visited the Galatian churches on each of his three missionary journeys. There is no mention in the epistle of another visit to the churches. The epistle was evidently Paul's last word to these churches, written after he had visited them on the third missionary journey.

GALATIANS—The people: The destination of this epistle has given rise to what is known as the North Galatian and the South Galatian theories. It seems more reasonable to suppose that it was sent to the churches in the area Paul visited on his first missionary journey, but this does not preclude the possibility that it had a wider circulation, even as far north as Pessinus, Ancyra, and Tavium. The word "Galatians" could be used in either an ethnographic sense, which would refer to the nationality of the people, or it could be used in a geographic sense, which would refer to the Roman province by that name. Regardless of the position taken, there is a common blood strain which identified people in that area where there was a mixture of population. The people for whom the province was named were Gauls, a Celtic tribe from the same stock that inhabited France. In the fourth century B.C. they invaded the Roman Empire and sacked Rome. Later they crossed into Greece and captured Delphi in 280 B.C. At the invitation of Nikomedes I, King of Bithynia, they crossed over into Asia Minor to help him in a civil war. They were warlike people and soon established themselves in Asia Minor. They were blond orientals. In 189 B.C. they were made subjects of the Roman Empire and became a province. Their boundaries varied, and for many years they retained their customs and language. The churches Paul established on his first missionary journey were included at one time in the territory of Galatia, and this is the name that Paul would normally give to these churches.

These Gallic Celts had much of the same temperament and characteristics of the American population. Caesar had this to say: "The infirmity of the Gauls is that they are fickle in their resolves, fond of change, and not to be trusted." Another described them as "frank, impetuous, impressible, eminently intelligent, fond of show, but extremely inconstant, the fruit of excessive vanity." Remember that they wanted to make Paul a god one day, and the next day they stoned him (see Acts 14).

Surely the Epistle to the Galatians has a message for us of like temper, who are beset on every hand by cults and isms innumerable that would take us, likewise, from our moorings in the gospel of grace.

GALATIANS—The epistle:

1 It is a stern, **severe**, and solemn message (Galatians 1:6-9; 3:1-5). It does not correct conduct, as the Corinthian letters do, but it is corrective—the Galatian believers were in grave peril. Because the foundations were being attacked, everything was threatened.

The epistle contains no word of commendation, praise, or thanksgiving. There is no request for prayer, and there is no mention of their standing in Christ. No one with him is mentioned by name (Galatians 1:2). Compare this with the other epistles of Paul.

2 The heart of Paul the apostle is laid bare, there is deep emotion and strong feeling. This is his **fighting epistle**—he has on his war paint. He has no toleration for legalism. Someone has said that Romans comes from the head of Paul while Galatians comes from his heart. "Galatians takes up controversially what Romans puts systematically."

3 It is the **declaration of emancipation** from legalism of any type. This was Martin Luther's favorite epistle, and it was on the masthead of the Reformation. It has been called the Magna Charta of the early church, the manifesto of Christian liberty, the impregnable citadel, and a veritable Gibraltar against any attack on the heart of the gospel. "Immortal victory is set upon its brow."

4 It is the strongest declaration and defense of the **doctrine of justification by faith** in or out of Scripture. It is God's polemic on behalf of the most vital truth of the Christian faith against any attack. Not only is a sinner saved by grace through faith, but the saved sinner lives by grace. Grace is a way *to* life and a way *of* life.

COMMENT: Galatians is God's polemic against legalism of every and any description. The Law is not discredited, despised, or disregarded. Its majesty, perfection, demands, fullness, and purpose are maintained. Yet these very qualities make it utterly impossible for man to come this route to God. Another way is opened—which entirely bypasses law—for man to be justified before God. The new route is by faith. Justification by faith is the theme, with the emphasis upon faith.

OUTLINE:

I. Introduction, Chapter 1:1-10

A. Salutation—cool greeting, vv. 1-5

B. Subject stated—warm declamation, vv. 6-10

II. Personal, Chapters 1:11– 2:14
Authority of the apostle and glory of the gospel

A. Experience of Paul in Arabia, Chapter 1:11-24

B. Experience of Paul with apostles in Jerusalem, Chapter 2:1-10

C. Experience of Paul in Antioch with Peter, Chapter 2:11-14

III. Doctrinal, Chapters 2:15–4:31
Justification by Faith
Faith vs. Works, Liberty vs. Bondage

A. Justification by faith—doctrine stated, Chapter 2:15-21

B. Justification by faith—experience of Galatians, Chapter 3:1-5

C. Justification by faith—illustration of Abraham, Chapter 3:6–4:18

D. Justification by faith—allegory of Hagar and Sarai, Chapter 4:19-31

IV. Practical, Chapters 5:1–6:10
Sanctification by the Spirit
Spirit vs. Flesh, Liberty vs. Bondage

A. Saved by faith and living by law perpetrates falling from grace, Chapter 5:1-15

B. Saved by faith and walking in the Spirit produces fruit of the Spirit, Chapter 5:16-26

C. Saved by faith and fruit of the Spirit presents Christian character, Chapter 6:1-10

V. Autographed conclusion, Chapter 6:11-18

A. Paul's own handwriting, v. 11

B. Paul's own testimony, vv. 12-18

   1. Cross of Christ vs. circumcision, vv. 12-15

   2. Christ's handwriting on Paul's body, vv. 16-18
     (The new circumcision of the new creation)

Ephesians

Ephesians

The Prison Epistles

A quartet of men left Rome in the year A.D. 62, bound for the province of Asia, which was located in what was designated as Asia Minor and is currently called Turkey. These men had on their persons four of the most sublime compositions of the Christian faith. These precious documents would be invaluable if the originals were in existence today. Rome did not comprehend the significance of the writings by an unknown prisoner. If she had, these men would have been apprehended and the documents seized.

When they bade farewell to the apostle Paul, each was given an epistle to bear to his particular constituency. These four letters are designated the "prison epistles of Paul," since he wrote them while imprisoned in Rome. He was awaiting a hearing before Nero who was the Caesar at that time. Paul, as a Roman citizen, had appealed his case to the emperor, and he was waiting to be heard.

Epaphroditus from Philippi (Philippians 4:18) had the Epistle to the Philippians.

Tychicus from Ephesus (Ephesians 6:21) had the Epistle to the Ephesians.

Epaphras from Colosse (Colossians 4:12) had the Epistle to the Colossians.

Onesimus (Philemon's slave) from Colosse (Philemon 10) had the Epistle to Philemon.

These epistles present a composite picture of Christ, the church, the Christian life, and the interrelationship and functioning of all three. These different facets present the Christian life on the highest plane.

EPHESIANS presents "the church, which is his body" (Ephesians 1:22, 23)—this is the invisible church, of which Christ is the head.

COLOSSIANS presents Christ who is "the head of the body, the church" (Colossians 1:18). The emphasis is upon Christ rather than on the church.

PHILIPPIANS presents Christian living, with Christ as the dynamic: "I can do all things through Christ, which strengtheneth me" (Philippians 4:13).

PHILEMON presents Christian living in action in a pagan society. "If thou count me, therefore, a partner, receive him as myself. If he hath wronged thee, or oweth thee [anything], put that on mine account" (Philemon 17, 18). The gospel walked in shoe leather in the first century—it worked.

In EPHESIANS, Christ is exalted above all things, God having "put all things under his feet" (Ephesians 1:22). Christ is the center of the circle of which the church is the periphery.

In COLOSSIANS, Christ is the fullness of God (*pleroma*). He is the periphery of the circle of which Christian living is the center (Colossians 2:9, 10).

In PHILIPPIANS, Christ is the center of the circle; Christian living is the periphery. The *kenosis* (emptying) is given (Philippians 2:5-8).

In PHILEMON, Christ is both the center and circumference: "Hearing of thy love and faith, which thou hast toward the Lord Jesus, and toward all saints" (Philemon 5).

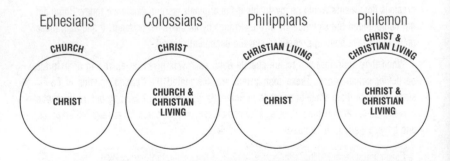

WRITER: Paul (Ephesians 1:1)

DATE: About A.D. 62. Paul arrived in Rome in A.D. 61 as a prisoner, and for two years he lived in his own hired house where he received those who came to him (Acts 28:16, 30).

THEME: Ephesians reveals the church as God's masterpiece (*poema*—see Ephesians 2:10), a mystery not revealed in the Old Testament. It is more wonderful than any temple made with hands, because it is constructed of living stones and indwelt by the Holy Spirit (2:20-22). It is the body of Christ in the world—to walk as He would walk and to wrestle against the wiles of the devil (1:22, 23; 4:1; 6:11, 12). Someday the church will leave the world and be presented to Christ as a bride (5:25-32).

Dr. Pierson called Ephesians "Paul's third-heaven epistle." Another has called it "the Alps of the New Testament." It is the Mt. Whitney of the High Sierras of all Scripture. This is the *Church Epistle*.

TITLE: The inscription *(en Epheso)* is omitted from the better manuscripts. It is thought that the Epistle to the Ephesians was a circular epistle, which included Ephesus and thereby explains the insertion of its name in some manuscripts. It is likewise thought that this epistle is the one to the Laodiceans referred to in Colossians 4:16. This could correspond to the last of the seven letters to the churches in Revelation 2 and 3 rather than to the first church. The contents of the Ephesian letter correspond more to the condition of the Ephesian church than to the one in Laodicea.

John Eadie concludes that this epistle is Paul's message to the church in Ephesus. He quotes from the testimony of the early church to sustain this thesis (Irenaeus, Clement of Alexandria, Origen, Tertullian, Cyprian).

Ephesians is the great church epistle, intended for all churches irrespective of geography, for the church is "one body" and its location is "in the heavenlies."

PAUL AND EPHESUS: The Holy Spirit forbade Paul, on his second missionary journey, to enter the province of Asia—where Ephesus was the prominent center (Acts 16:6). He traveled west until he came to the sea, where it was necessary for God, by means of a vision, to direct him to Macedonia. He was led by the Spirit into Europe as far as Corinth, after which he returned by way of Ephesus (Acts 18:19).

Being favorably impressed by the opportunities for missionary work, he promised to return. This he did on the third missionary journey. He discovered that another, by the name of Apollos, had been there in the interval between his second and third missionary journeys; but Apollos had preached only the baptism of John—not the gospel of grace. Paul began a ministry there that was far-reaching. For two years he spoke in the school of Tyrannus, and the gospel penetrated into every center of the province of Asia. Evidently, it was at this time that the churches addressed in Revelation 2 and 3 were founded as a result of this ministry of Paul.

This was probably the "high water mark" in the missionary labors of Paul. He considered Ephesus his great opportunity and stayed there longer than in any other place. The people of Ephesus heard more Bible teaching from Paul than did any other people, which is the reason he could write to them the deep truths contained in this epistle.

He met great opposition (1 Corinthians 16:8, 9), but God marvelously preserved him, which encouraged him to continue (see Acts 19:23-41). Paul loved this church in Ephesus. His last meeting with the Ephesian elders was a tender farewell (see Acts 20:17-38).

Ephesus was the principal city of Asia Minor—and probably of the entire eastern section of the Roman Empire. It was virile and aggressive at this time, while the culture of Athens was decadent, and the commercialism of Corinth was corroded with immorality.

OUTLINE:

I. **Doctrinal,** Chapters 1–3
   The **heavenly calling** of the church (vocalization)

   A. The church is a BODY, Chapter 1

   1. Introduction, vv. 1, 2

   2. God the Father **planned** the church, vv. 3-6
      "A body hast thou prepared me" (Hebrews 10:5)

   3. God the Son **paid** the price for the church, vv. 7-12
      "Redemption through his blood" (v. 7)

   4. God the Holy Spirit **protects** the church, vv. 13, 14
      "By one Spirit were we all baptized into one body"
      (1 Corinthians 12:13)

   5. **Prayer** for knowledge and power, vv. 15-23

   B. The church is a TEMPLE, Chapter 2

   1. The **material** for construction, vv. 1-10
      Those "dead in trespasses" (v. 1) are made into a
      living temple

   2. The **method** of construction, vv. 11-18

   3. The **meaning** of the construction *(quo animo),* vv. 19-22
      "Groweth unto an holy temple in the Lord" (v. 21)

   C. The church is a MYSTERY, Chapter 3

   1. The **explanation** of the mystery, vv. 1-4
      Not revealed in the Old Testament

   2. The **definition** of the mystery, vv. 5-13
      Jews and Gentiles are partakers of the same body—
      the church

   3. **Prayer** for power and knowledge, vv. 14-21
      "Strengthened with might" (v. 16) and "to know the love of
      Christ" (v. 19)

II. **Practical,** Chapters 4–6
    The **earthly conduct** of the church (vocation)

    A. The church is a NEW MAN, Chapter 4

    1. The **exhibition** of the new man, vv. 1-6
       "Endeavoring to keep the unity of the Spirit" (v. 3)

2. The **inhibition** of the new man, vv. 7-16
*"No more children"(v. 14); "grow up into him"(v. 15);
"perfect man" (v. 13)*

3. The **prohibition** of the new man, vv. 17-32
*"Walk not as other Gentiles walk" (v. 17); "be ye kind one
to another" (v. 32)*

B. The church will be a BRIDE, Chapter 5

1. The **engagement** of the church, vv. 1-17
*"For I have espoused you to one husband that I may present
you as a chaste virgin to Christ" (2 Corinthians 11:2)*

2. The **experience** of the church, vv. 18-24
"Be filled with the Spirit" (v. 18)

3. The **expectation** of the church, vv. 25-33
"That he might present it to himself a glorious church" (v. 27)

C. The church is a SOLDIER, Chapter 6

1. The soldier's **relationships**, vv. 1-9
*"No man that warreth entangleth himself with the affairs of
this life" (2 Timothy 2:4)*

2. The soldier's **enemy**, vv. 10-12
"The wiles of the devil" (v. 11)

3. The soldier's **protection**, vv. 13-18
The whole armour of God" (v. 13)

4. The soldier's **example**—Paul, a good soldier of Jesus
Christ, vv. 19-22

5. The soldier's **benediction**, vv. 23, 24

Philippians

Philippians

THE EARTHLY WALK OF A HEAVENLY PEOPLE

WRITER: Paul (Philippians 1:1)

DATE: A.D. 62; written at the same time as Ephesians, it is one of the prison epistles.

CITY OF PHILIPPI: Philippi was a Roman colony. Although it was a miniature of Rome and imitated and aped Rome in every way, it was nonetheless a city which had a higher cultural level than other cities visited by Paul.

CHURCH OF PHILIPPI:

1 It was less Jewish and more Gentile than were all others (the names of individuals mentioned are Greek and Roman). This was the first church established in Europe (Acts 16:6-40), which gives special meaning to Gentiles.

2 Women occupied a prominent place in this church. Paul attended, first of all, not the synagogue, but a prayer meeting of women (Acts 16:12-15). A woman named Lydia was the first convert in Europe. Two women were prominent in the church (Philippians 4:2), and there were others who labored in the church (Philippians 4:3).

3 It was generous in its gifts to the Lord's work (Philippians 4:10-16). Paul cited them as examples to others in giving (2 Corinthians 8:1-5).

OCCASION FOR EPISTLE:

There were two specific circumstances that occasioned the writing of this epistle:

1 The church at Philippi had been generous in support of Paul, and he wrote this letter to thank them. When he was in prison in Rome, they sent help by the hands of Epaphroditus. Epaphroditus became ill in Rome, and when he recovered, Paul wrote this letter and sent it by the messenger who had brought him help.

2 A deeper reason was evidently the division that was arising because of the misunderstanding between two of the women (Philippians 4:2). One of the phrases that Paul used again and again is "you all," speaking to and of all the believers in the church.

KEY: The epistle is practical; its key thought is *joy*. It has been labeled "The Secret of Joy." Some form of the word occurs 19 times. It answers the question, "How may I have joy in my heart?" The man who wrote, "Rejoice in the Lord always: and again I say, Rejoice" (Philippians 4:4), was in the Mamertine prison in Rome. Joy does not depend upon circumstances.

OUTLINE:

I.   PHILOSOPHY for Christian living, Chapter 1

A. Introduction, vv. 1, 2

B. Paul's tender feeling for the Philippians, vv. 3-11

C. Bonds and afflictions further the gospel, vv. 12-20

D. In life or death—Christ, vv. 21-30

II.   PATTERN for Christian living, Chapter 2
(Key verses: 5-11)

A. Others, vv. 1-4

B. Mind of Christ—humble, vv. 5-8

C. Mind of God—exaltation of Christ, vv. 9-11

D. Mind of Paul—things of Christ, vv. 12-18

E. Mind of Timothy—like-minded with Paul, vv. 19-24

F. Mind of Epaphroditus—the work of Christ, vv. 25-30

III.   PRIZE for Christian living, Chapter 3
(Key verses: 10-14)

A. Paul changed his bookkeeping system of the past, vv. 1-9

B. Paul changed his purpose for the present, vv. 10-19

C. Paul changed his hope for the future, vv. 20, 21

IV.   POWER for Christian living, Chapter 4
(Key verse: 13)

A. Joy—the source of power, vv. 1-4

B. Prayer—the secret of power, vv. 5-7

C. Contemplation of Christ—the sanctuary of power, vv. 8, 9

D. In Christ—the satisfaction of power, vv. 10-23

Colossians

Colossians

WRITER: Paul (Colossians 1:1)

DATE: About A.D. 62

CHURCH AT COLOSSE: Paul had never been to Colosse when he wrote this epistle (Colossians 2:1). He was in Ephesus for about two years where he had his most fruitful ministry (Acts 19:8-19). Colosse was 75 to 100 miles east of Ephesus, and visitors from Colosse had heard Paul and had come to know Christ. Apparently Philemon was one of these. A church came into existence in Colosse (Philemon 2), and Epaphras was the minister (Colossians 1:4-8; 4:12, 13). Paul intended to visit there when he was released from prison (Philemon 22). Paul wrote to this church as though it were his own.

PROBLEM AT COLOSSE: Colosse, located in southwest Phrygia in Asia Minor near Laodicea, was beset with oriental mysticism. Gnosticism had evidently intruded with its Greek pantheistic philosophy of the demiurge.

GNOSTICISM	PAUL'S ANSWER
1 – They had an exclusive spirit (were aristocratic in wisdom).	Col. 1:28
2 – They held speculative tenets on creation—that God did not create the universe directly, but created a creature who in turn created another creature, until one finally created the physical universe. Christ was considered a creature in this long series of creations.	Col. 1:15-19; 2:18
3 – Their ethical practice was asceticism (influenced by Greek Stoicism) and unrestrained licentiousness (from Greek Epicureanism).	Col. 2:16, 23 Col. 3:5-9

MESSAGE OF COLOSSIANS: Colossians is the chart and compass that enable the believer to sail between the ever-present Scylla and Charybdis. "Pure Christianity lives between two dangers ever present: the danger that it will evaporate into a philosophy—philosophies of the atonement ... and the danger that it will freeze into a form" (Dr. Scofield). Jesus said that He is the water of life. He did not say that He was the ice of life; He did not say that He was the steam of life. We are not told to add something to Christ nor to subtract from Him.

The message of this epistle can best be seen by comparing it with other prison epistles.

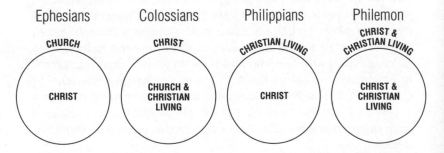

SUBJECT:	
Ephesians	The body of believers, called the church, of which Christ is the Head
Colossians	The Head of the body who is Christ; the body is only secondary (Colossians 1:18)

THEME:

Philippians	Christian living is the theme and the periphery of the circle where Christ is the center.
Colossians	Christ is the theme and the periphery of the circle where Christian living is the center.

Philippians emphasizes the *kenosis*—Christ became a Servant (Philippians 2:7).

Colossians emphasizes the *pleroma*—Christ is the fullness of God (Colossians 2:9).

"Thou, O Christ, art all I want; more than all in Thee I find" (Charles Wesley).

OUTLINE:

I. **DOCTRINAL,** Chapters 1, 2
    In Christ, the fullness (pleroma) of God, we are made full.

    A. Introduction, Chapter 1:1-8

    B. Paul's prayer, Chapter 1:9-14

    C. Person of Christ, Chapter 1:15-19

    D. Objective work of Christ for sinners, Chapter 1:20-23

    E. Subjective work of Christ for saints, Chapter 1:24-29

    F. Christ, the answer to philosophy, Chapter 2:1-15
       (for the HEAD)

    G. Christ, the answer to ritual, Chapter 2:16-23
       (for the HEART)

II. **PRACTICAL,** Chapters 3, 4
    Christ, the fullness of God, poured out in life through believers.
    (Breaking the alabaster box of ointment in the world.)

    A. Thoughts and affections of believers are heavenly, Chapter 3:1-4
       (The believer's heart should be in heaven where his Head is.)

    B. Living of believers is holy, Chapters 3:5–4:6
       (In all relationships—personal, social, marital, parental, capital and labor—the believer should manifest Christ.)

    C. Fellowship of believers is hearty, Chapter 4:7-18
       (Roster of faithful workers similar to Romans 16 and Hebrews 11.)

Thessalonians

1 Thessalonians

WRITER: Paul

DATE: A.D. 52-53

PLACE: Thessalonica was a Roman colony and very important in the life of the Roman Empire. It was located 100 miles west of Philippi and about 200 miles north of Athens. It was the chief city of Macedonia. Cicero said, "Thessalonica is in the bosom of the Empire." It was first named Therma because of hot springs in that area. In 316 B.C. Cassander (who succeeded Alexander the Great) named it in memory of his wife, Thessalonike, a half-sister of Alexander the Great. Thessalonica is still in existence, and the present-day name is Salonika.

The church in Thessalonica was a model church. Paul cited it to the Corinthians as an example (see 1 Thessalonians 1:7; 2 Corinthians 8:1-5).

OCCASION: This was the earliest epistle written by Paul. It was written from Athens or, more likely, Corinth on his second missionary journey. Paul had to leave Thessalonica "posthaste" due to the great opposition to the gospel. The enemy pursued him to Berea, and again Paul was forced to leave. He left Silas and Timothy at Berea and went on to Athens. It was evidently there that Timothy brought him word from the church in Thessalonica (1 Thessalonians 3:6), together with some questions that they had raised. Paul wrote his first epistle in response to their overture.

THEME: Although Paul was in Thessalonica less than a month (Acts 17:2), he touched on many of the great doctrines of the church. Among them was the second coming of Christ. This theme was not above the heads of the new converts, according to the great apostle. The particular phase in the second coming of Christ which he emphasized was Christ's coming for believers. The second coming of Christ in relationship to believers is a comfort (1 Thessalonians 4:18). This aspect is quite different from His catastrophic and cataclysmic coming in glory to establish His kingdom by putting down all unrighteousness (Revelation 19:11-16).

PURPOSE:

1 – To *confirm* young converts in the elementary truth of the gospel.

2 – To *condition* them to go on unto holy living.

3 – To *comfort* them regarding the return of Christ.

A heathen inscription in Thessalonica read: "After death no reviving, after the grave no meeting again."

OUTLINE:

I. **The Christian's ATTITUDE toward the return of Christ,** Chapter 1
(to serve ... to wait ..., vv. 9, 10)

II. **The Christian's REWARD at the return of Christ,** Chapter 2

III. **The Christian's LIFE and the return of Christ,** Chapters 3:1—4:12

IV. **The Christian's DEATH and the return of Christ,** Chapter 4:13-18

V. **The Christian's ACTIONS in view of the return of Christ,** Chapter 5
(Note 22 specific commands to Christians, beginning at v. 11.)

For this book I suggest two outlines. Each gives a needed emphasis that is not in the other.

I. **Coming of Christ is an INSPIRING HOPE,** Chapter 1

A. Introduction, vv. 1-4

B. Gospel received in much assurance and much affliction, vv. 5-7

C. Gospel results, vv. 8-10

II. **Coming of Christ is a WORKING HOPE,** Chapter 2

A. Motive and method of a true witness for Christ, vv. 1-6

B. Mother side of the apostle's ministry (comfort), vv. 7-9

C. Father side of the apostle's ministry (charge), vv. 10-13

D. Brother side of the apostle's ministry (challenge), vv. 14-16

E. Reward of a true witness for Christ, vv. 17-20

III. **Coming of Christ is a PURIFYING HOPE,** Chapters 3:1—4:12

A. Timothy brings a good report of Thessalonians, Chapter 3:1-8

B. Paul urges Thessalonians to continue to grow in faith, Chapter 3:9-13

C. How believers are to walk, Chapter 4:1-12

IV. **Coming of Christ is a COMFORTING HOPE,** Chapter 4:13-18
(What death means to a Christian; what the Rapture means to the church.)

V. **Coming of Christ is a ROUSING HOPE (leads to action),** Chapter 5
(Dead believers are asleep in Jesus; living believers are awake for Jesus.)

A. Call to be awake and alert in view of Christ's coming, vv. 1-10

B. Commandments for Christians, vv. 11-28

2 Thessalonians

2 Thessalonians

WRITER: Paul

DATE: A.D. 52-53 (The second epistle followed shortly after the first.)

OCCASION: The first letter to the Thessalonians gave rise to further questions, and Paul is attempting to answer these. There was circulating in the Thessalonian church a letter or report, purported to have come from Paul, which was inclined to disturb the Christians. This false report claimed that Christ had already come and had already gathered out the church to Himself and that the world was then living in the judgments of the "day of the Lord." Their present persecutions confirmed this false report. Paul attempts to allay their fears by stating definitely that "our gathering together unto him" is yet future (2 Thessalonians 2:1) and that "the day of the Lord" has certain forerunners which must first come. The apostasy and the "man of sin" must come first; the removal of the remnant of believers at "our gathering together unto him" makes the apostasy in the professing church 100% (Luke 18:8). Every era of persecution or trouble has given rise to the false impression that the church is going through the time of judgment which Christ identified as the "great tribulation" (Matthew 24:21). This period has been so clearly identified by Christ that there is no reason for getting panicky or being stampeded into an unwarranted position. Christ said that there is coming a small interval which will be blocked off by "such as was not since the beginning of the world to this time, no, nor ever shall be" (Matthew 24:21). Nothing like it has taken place before, and nothing like it will ever take place afterward. Has there ever been such a period of unparalleled trouble? The answer is obvious.

THEME: The first epistle to the Thessalonians deals with the Rapture, Christ's coming for believers. The second epistle relates the return of Christ to that phase where He returns to the earth in judgment and where one of the accomplishments is in connection with the "man of sin," whom He "shall destroy with the brightness of his coming" (2 Thessalonians 2:8). These two aspects are clearly delineated. The interval between these two phases is the Great Tribulation, which can be further identified with the 70th week of Daniel 9 as a period of seven years.

THE DAY OF THE LORD: This is the phrase which occurs in 2 Thessalonians 2:2 (incorrectly translated "the day of Christ" in the Authorized Version). It is an Old Testament phrase with definite connotations. It occurs in the writings of the Old Testament prophets where it relates to the future kingdom promised in the Old Testament. The day of Christ is a New Testament expression (1 Corinthians 1:8); it relates here to the future of the church. The day of the Lord is connected with the coming of Christ as it relates to the setting up of the kingdom. The day of Christ is connected with the coming of Christ for the church. Whatever else is implied in these two statements, certainly this is basic. The teaching in 1 Thessalonians is that the saints who have died will have part in Christ's coming for His living saints; in 2 Thessalonians it is that the saints who are alive will not have part in the Great Tribulation. The return of Christ has a peculiar and precious meaning for His saints.

OUTLINE:

I. PERSECUTION of believers now; judgment of unbelievers hereafter (at coming of Christ), Chapter 1

A. Introduction, vv. 1, 2

B. Persecution of believers and fruits of it, vv. 3-7

C. Judgment of wicked at coming of Christ, vv. 8-12

II. PROGRAM for world in connection with coming of Christ, Chapter 2:1-12

A. Rapture occurs first, v. 1

B. Day of the Lord follows; introduced by total apostasy and appearance of man of sin, vv. 2-5

C. Mystery of lawlessness working today; lawless one restrained by Holy Spirit, vv. 6-8

D. Lawless one to appear in Great Tribulation Period, vv. 9-12

III. PRACTICALITY of coming of Christ, Chapters 2:13–3:18

A. Believers should be established in the WORD, Chapter 2:13-17

B. Believers should be established in their WALK, Chapter 3:1-7

C. Believers should be established in their WORK, Chapter 3:8-18

Timothy

Timothy

Pastoral Epistles

The two letters to Timothy and the one to Titus are labeled Pastoral Epistles. The contents of the letters reveal the obvious reason for this. They were written by Paul to two of his young converts (1 Timothy 1:2; Titus 1:4) who had followed him on many of his missionary journeys and whom he had established as pastors of churches at the time of the writing of these epistles. Although they were addressed by Paul to his young friends in the ministry, the message is for churches. He gave instructions for the orderly procedure of local and visible churches. These letters have a particular message to young pastors, and they have pertinent instructions for the present-day church.

WRITER: Paul

DATE: About A.D. 64. Probably Paul was released from prison at Rome between A.D. 64 and 67. If this is accurate, it was during this interval that he wrote this first letter to Timothy. He wrote to Titus at this same time. Some authorities think that Paul wrote from Macedonia. Apparently he had left Timothy in Ephesus (1 Timothy 1:3), and he wrote this letter to encourage and assist him (1 Timothy 6:20).

THEME: Government and order in the local church. This is in contrast to the Epistle to the Ephesians where the church is the body of Christ, the invisible church. Here it is a local assembly of believers organized for a common purpose.

KEY VERSES: 1 Timothy 1:3 and 3:15. Sound doctrine and correct conduct identify the local church. "Doctrine" occurs eight times; "godliness" occurs eight times; "teach" and "teacher" occur seven times; "good" occurs 22 times.

OUTLINE:

I. Faith of the church, Chapter 1

A. Introduction, vv. 1, 2

B. Warning against unsound doctrine, vv. 3-10

C. Personal testimony of Paul, vv. 11-17

D. Charge to Timothy, vv. 18-20

II. Public prayer and woman's place in the churches, Chapter 2

A. Public prayer for the public and public officials, vv. 1-7

B. How men are to pray, v. 8

C. How women are to pray, vv. 9-15

III. Officers in the churches, Chapter 3

A. Requirements for elders, vv. 1-7

B. Requirements for deacons, vv. 8-13

C. Report of Paul to Timothy, vv. 14-16

IV. Apostasy in the churches, Chapter 4

A. How to recognize the apostates, vv. 1-5

B. What the "good minister" can do in times of apostasy, vv. 6-16

V. Duties of officers of the churches, Chapters 5, 6

A. Relationship of ministers to different groups in the local church, Chapter 5

B. Relationship of believers to others, Chapter 6

2 Timothy

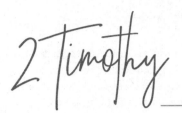

WRITER: Paul

DATE: A.D. 67. The following is a probable calendar of the events of Paul's life during his last years:

A.D. 58	Paul's arrest in Jerusalem.
A.D. 61	His arrival in Rome.
A.D. 61-63	His first Roman imprisonment.
A.D. 64-67	His release. He writes 1 Timothy and Titus, probably from Macedonia
A.D. 67-68	His arrest and death. He writes 2 Timothy prior to his death in Rome.

KEY VERSES: 2 Timothy 2:15 and 4:2. Key words are "ashamed" (1:8, 12) and "endure" (2:3).

THEME: Loyalty in days of apostasy.

1 – Loyalty in suffering (Chapter 1)
2 – Loyalty in service (Chapter 2)
3 – Loyalty in apostasy (Chapters 3:1—4:5)
4 – Loyalty of the Lord to His servants in desertion (Chapter 4:6-22)

REMARKS: Webster's definition of apostasy is: total desertion of principles of faith. Apostasy is not due to ignorance; it is a heresy. Apostasy is deliberate error; it is intentional departure from the faith. An apostate is one who knows the truth of the gospel (doctrines of the faith).

In 2 Timothy, Paul speaks of the ultimate outcome of gospel preaching. The final fruition will not be the total conversion of mankind, nor will it usher in the Millennium. On the contrary, there will come about an apostasy which will well-nigh blot out "the faith" from the earth. This is in complete harmony with the startling word of Christ, "When the Son of man cometh, shall he find faith on the earth?" (Luke 18:8). This is not in keeping, of course, with a social gospel which expects to transform the world by tinkering with the social system. These vain optimists have no patience with the doleful words of 2 Timothy. Nevertheless, the cold and hard facts of history and the events of the present hour demonstrate the accuracy of Paul. We are now in the midst of an apostasy which is cut to the pattern of Paul's words in remarkable detail.

Although the visible church has entered the orbit of awful apostasy, the invisible church is on its way to the epiphany of glory.

SPECIAL FEATURE: "Swan Song" of the Apostle. The deathbed statement of any individual has an importance that is not attached to other remarks. This is what lends significance to 2 Timothy. It is the deathbed communication of Paul; it is his final message. It has a note of sadness that is not detected in his other epistles. Nevertheless, there is the overtone of triumph, "I have fought a good fight, I have finished my course ...." Paul writes his own epitaph in 4:6-8. The epistle is very personal—there are 25 references to individuals.

OUTLINE:

I.   Afflictions of the gospel, Chapter 1

  A. Introduction, vv. 1-7

  B. Not ashamed, but a partaker of affliction, vv. 8-11

  C. Not ashamed, but assured, vv. 12-18

II.   Active in service, Chapter 2

  A. A son, vv. 1, 2

  B. A good soldier, vv. 3, 4

  C. An athlete, v. 5

  D. A farmer, vv. 6-14

  E. A workman, vv. 15-19

  F. A vessel, vv. 20-23

  G. A servant, vv. 24-26

III. Apostasy coming; authority of the Scriptures, Chapters 3:1—4:5

  A. Conditions in the last days, Chapter 3:1-9

  B. Authority of Scriptures in the last days, Chapter 3:10-17

  C. Instructions for the last days, Chapter 4:1-5

IV.   Allegiance to the Lord and of the Lord, Chapter 4:6-22

  A. Deathbed testimony of Paul, vv. 6-8

  B. Last words, vv. 9-22
  ("The Lord stood with me.")

Titus

Titus

WRITER: Paul

DATE: A.D. 64-67 (See notes on 1 Timothy.)

CONTRAST: While little is known of either Timothy or Titus, there seems to have been quite a contrast between them. Titus seems to have been a stronger man, both physically and spiritually, since Paul expresses less concern for his welfare. Titus was probably more mature and possessed a virile personality. Timothy was a Jew who was circumcised by Paul, but Titus was a Gentile, and Paul seems to have refused to circumcise him (Galatians 2:3). Paul circumcised one young preacher and refused to circumcise the other. Surely there is no rule that can be drawn from this other than "in Christ Jesus neither circumcision availeth any thing, nor uncircumcision, but a new creature" (Galatians 6:15).

THE NEW TESTAMENT CHURCH: Here is a fine picture of the New Testament church in its full-orbed realization in the community as an organization. Many boast today that they belong to a New Testament church. In this epistle is found the measuring rod. The ideal church is one that has an orderly organization, is sound in doctrine, pure in life, and "ready to every good work" (Titus 3:1).

THE RETURN OF CHRIST: In the first two epistles that Paul wrote (1 and 2 Thessalonians), the return of Christ is a great pulsing hope. This has led some critics to say that Paul believed this only when he was young and that he changed when he became more mature. However, in this epistle to Titus, one of his last, the blessed hope still possesses the soul of this intrepid pioneer of faith, "Looking for that blessed hope, and the glorious appearing of the great God and our Saviour, Jesus Christ" (Titus 2:13). The word for "looking" has the root meaning of *entertaining*. This is the hope that occupied the guest chamber in the heart of Paul during all of his life, beginning at the Damascus Road and going on to the Appian Way.

OUTLINE:

I. **The church is an organization,** Chapter 1
   (As such, it should be orderly [v. 5].)

   A. Introduction, vv. 1-4

   B. An orderly church must have ordained elders who meet prescribed requirements, vv. 5-9

   C. The bad reputation of the Cretans, vv. 10-16

II. **The church is to teach and preach the Word of God,** Chapter 2

   A. The church must teach sound doctrine, vv. 1-10

   B. The church must preach the grace of God, vv. 11-15

III. **The church is to perform good works,** Chapter 3
   (To do this, it should be eager, anxious, and learning to perform good works [vv. 1, 8, 14].)

   A. Good works are evidence of salvation, vv. 1-7
   (The work of the Holy Spirit in contrast to the old life.)

   B. Good works are profitable for the present and future, vv. 8-15

Philemon

Philemon

WRITER: Paul

DATE: Probably A.D. 62 (See outline of Ephesians and the Prison Epistles introduction.)

FORM: The Epistles present a different style in revelation. God used law, history, poetry, prophecy, and the Gospels heretofore, but in the Epistles He adopted a more personal and direct method. In this intimate way, He looks back to the Cross and talks about the church. Someone has said that the Epistles are the love letters of Christ to us. Dr. Deissmann divided them into two classifications: Epistles and letters. The Epistles are general, while the letters are more personal and individual. Under this division, the Epistle of Philemon would be classified as a letter, for it is individual and intimate. There is reason to believe that Paul did not expect its contents to be divulged (at other times he knew that he was writing Scripture). This does not detract from the inspiration and value of Philemon, but rather enhances its value and message.

BACKGROUND: The story behind the Epistle to Philemon was enacted on the black background of slavery. There were approximately 60 million slaves in the Roman Empire, where the total population did not exceed 120 million. A slave was a chattel. He was treated worse than an enemy and was subject to the whim of his master. The story can be briefly reconstructed. Onesimus was a slave belonging to Philemon, a Christian of Colosse. This slave had opportunity to run away and seized on it. He made his way to Rome where he expected his identity and past life to be swallowed up by the great metropolis. One day he chanced upon a gathering where Paul was preaching. There he heard the gospel of the Lord Jesus Christ, and the Holy Spirit regenerated him, making him a new creature in Christ. He told his story to Paul, and Paul sent him back to Philemon with this accompanying letter.

PURPOSE: The **primary** purpose of this epistle is to reveal Christ's love for us in what He did for us before God in pleading our case. This is the finest illustration of substitution: "If he hath wronged thee, or oweth thee [anything], put that on mine account" (Philemon 18). We can hear Christ agreeing to take our place and to have all our sin imputed to Him—"For he hath made him ... to be sin for us ..." (2 Corinthians 5:21). He took our place in death, but He gives us His place in life: "If thou count me, therefore, a partner, receive him as myself" (Philemon 17). We have the standing of Christ before God, or we have none at all. He took our hell, and He gives us His heaven "that we might be made the righteousness of God in him" (2 Corinthians 5:21). Onesimus, an unprofitable runaway slave, was to be received as Paul, the great apostle, would have been received in the home of Philemon.

The **practical** purpose is to teach brotherly love. Paul spoke of the new relationship between master and servant in the other Prison Epistles. Here he demonstrates how it should work. These men, belonging to two different classes in the Roman Empire, hating each other and hurting each other, are now brothers in Christ—and they are to act like it. This is the only solution to the problem of capital and labor.

OUTLINE:

Hebrews

Hebrews

Paul (?). Although the Authorized Version has the heading, "Epistle of Paul the Apostle to the Hebrews," there is still a question as to authorship. The American Revised Version corrects this and gives the heading, "The Epistle to the Hebrews." In spite of the fact that the Pauline authorship cannot be confirmed in a dogmatic fashion, there is abundant evidence that Paul was the author. Both internal and external evidence support the authorship of Paul. The writer had been in bonds (10:34); he wrote from Italy (13:24); his companion was Timothy (13:23). The writing is Pauline and, in my opinion, Peter identifies Paul as the writer (2 Peter 3:15, 16; cf. 1 Peter 1:1).

DATE: Hebrews 10:11 reveals that it was written before the destruction of the temple by Titus in A.D. 70.

THEME: Coleridge said that Romans revealed the *necessity* of the Christian faith, but that Hebrews revealed the *superiority* of the Christian faith. This thought is expressed in the use of the comparative word "better," which occurs 13 times. Here are some other words that express the theme:

> "Perfect"—occurs 15 times (cognate words);
>
> "Let us"—occurs 13 times;
>
> "Let"—occurs five times.

Two verses, likewise, convey this "better" way: Hebrews 3:1 and 12:3.

OUTLINE:

I. **Christ better than Old Testament economy,** Chapters 1– 10
   (Doctrinal)

A. Christ is superior to prophets, Chapter 1:1-3

B. Christ is superior to angels, Chapters 1:4–2:18

    1. Deity of Christ, Chapter 1:4-14

    2. Humanity of Christ, Chapter 2
   First Danger Signal: Peril of drifting, Chapter 2:1-4

C. Christ is superior to Moses, Chapters 3:1–4:2
   Second Danger Signal: Peril of doubting, Chapters 3:7—4:2

D. Christ is superior to Joshua, Chapter 4:3-13

E. Christ is superior to the Levitical priesthood, Chapters 4:14–7:28

    1. Our great High Priest, Chapter 4:14-16

    2. Definition of a priest, Chapter 5:1-10
   Third Danger Signal: Peril of dull hearing, Chapter 5:11-14

    3. *Fourth Danger Signal: Peril of departing, Chapter 6*

    4. Christ our High Priest after order of Melchizedek, Chapter 7

        a. Christ is perpetual Priest, vv. 1-3

        b. Christ is perfect Priest, vv. 4-22

        c. Christ in His Person is perpetual and perfect Priest, vv. 23-28

F. Christ as our High Priest ministers in superior sanctuary by better covenant built upon better promises, Chapters 8–10

    1. True tabernacle, Chapter 8:1-5

    2. New covenant better than the old, Chapter 8:6-13

    3. New sanctuary better than the old, Chapter 9:1-10

James

General Epistles

James; 1 and 2 Peter; 1, 2 and 3 John; and Jude are designated as "catholic" epistles in the sense of "universal," because they are not addressed to a particular individual or church, but to the church as a whole.

WRITER: James. The problem of authorship is a major one. Some find at least four men by the name of James in the New Testament. At least three are clearly identified:

1 James, brother of John, son of Zebedee, called by our Lord "son of thunder" (Mark 3:17). He was slain by Herod (Acts 12:1, 2).

2 James, son of Alphaeus, called "James the less" (Mark 15:40). He is mentioned in the list of apostles, but very little is known concerning him.

3 James, the Lord's brother (Matthew 13:55; Mark 6:3), in reality a half-brother according to the flesh. He became head of the church at Jerusalem (Acts 15:13). This James is evidently the writer of this epistle (Galatians 2:9).

DATE: A.D. 45-50. This was the first book of the New Testament to be written. Some have taken the position that James wrote to combat the writings of Paul. It is obvious that this is an erroneous position, since none of Paul's epistles were in existence at the time of this writing.

JAMES AND PAUL: The seeming contradiction between James and Paul can be easily explained when the message of James is considered. James takes the position, as does Paul, that we are justified by faith but that the faith which justifies produces good works. Calvin said, "Faith alone saves, but the faith that saves is not alone." Justification is shown by works—not justified *by*, but *for*, good works. James and Paul present the two aspects of justification by faith.

Paul emphasized both phases:

Faith—not justified *by* works (Ephesians 2:8, 9 and Titus 3:5)
Works—justified *for* works (Ephesians 2:10 and Titus 3:8)

Faith is the root of salvation—works are the fruit of salvation. Faith is the cause of salvation—works are the result of salvation.

KEY VERSES: James 1:22 and 2:20

THEME: Ethics of Christianity, not doctrine. The Epistle of James has been compared to the book of Proverbs in the Old Testament. Both emphasize the practical. In both there is the learning experience for the child of God.

Justification by faith is demonstrated by works. Justification by faith is poured into the test tube of:

Works—Chapters 1, 2		Worldliness—Chapter 4
Words—Chapter 3		Warning to the rich—Chapter 5

OUTLINE:

I. Verification of genuine faith, Chapters 1–3

   A. God tests faith by trials, Chapter 1:1-12
   (Twofold result: development of patience here, v. 3; reward hereafter, v. 12)

   B. God does not test faith with evil, Chapter 1:13-21
   (Evil comes from within—the flesh, v. 14)

   C. God tests faith by the Word, not by man's words, Chapter 1:22-27
   (Doing, not doctrine, is the final test of faith; knowing is not enough.)

   D. God tests faith by attitude and action in respect of persons, Chapter 2:1-13

   E. God tests faith by good works, Chapter 2:14-26
   (Abraham is an illustration of works, v. 21)

   F. God tests faith by the tongue, Chapter 3
   ("What is in the well of the heart will come up through the bucket of the mouth.")

II. Vacuity and vapidness of worldliness, Chapter 4
   (Worldliness is identified with fighting and the spirit of dissension, vv. 1, 2)

III. Vexation of the rich; value of the imminent coming of Christ, Chapter 5
   (The soon coming of Christ produces patience, vv. 7, 8, and prayer, vv. 13-18)

   A. Riches are a care (rich warned), vv. 1-6

   B. Coming of Christ is a comfort, vv. 7-12

   C. Prayer of the righteous is a power, vv. 13-20

1 Peter

1 Peter

WRITER: Simon Peter (1 Peter 1:1). Peter has been called the ignorant fisherman, but no man who had spent three years in the school of Jesus could be called ignorant, and the epistles of Peter confirm this.

A great change is seen in the life of Peter from these epistles. He had been impetuous, but now he is patient. The transforming power of the gospel has wrought this change in his life.

DATE: A.D. 64-67. Peter wrote his two epistles and was put to death sometime during this period. First Peter was written, evidently, around A.D. 64 and 2 Peter a short time later.

PLACE: Although the place from which it was written has been the preeminent problem of this epistle, it is given as Babylon (1 Peter 5:13). Many treat this in a metaphorical sense as meaning Rome. However, the legend that Peter was in Rome for 25 years preceding his martyrdom is grounded in the apocryphal writings of the heretical Ebionites.

The list of countries in 1 Peter 1:1 is from east to west, which suggests that the writer was in the East at the time of writing. Furthermore, Babylon is directly mentioned as the origin, and this epistle was written before Rome was called Babylon in a symbolic way in the book of Revelation. Also, the direct manner of Peter's writing, to the extent of bluntness, contradicts the theory that he used Babylon in a symbolic way. If Peter had meant Rome, the chances are that he would have said *Rome*. There was at this time a large colony of Jews in ancient Babylon who had fled Rome due to severe persecution under Claudius, and at the time of writing bloody Nero was on the throne. This is in harmony with the theme of the epistle. In spite of the fact that Papias mentions the death of Peter as occurring in Rome, there is no substantial historical basis for this supposition.

THEME: Christian hope in the time of trial.

Peter deals with doctrine and handles weighty subjects. This is seen in his treatment of the great words of the gospel, many of which are gathered together at the outset (1 Peter 1:2)—elect, foreknowledge, sanctification, obedience, blood, and the Trinity. He used some of these words several times. Added to these are: salvation (used three times), revelation (with cognate words, used five times), glory (with cognate words, used 16 times), faith (five times), and hope (four times). Peter has been called the *apostle of hope*; Paul, the *apostle of faith*; John, the *apostle of love*.

The word that conveys the theme, however, is *suffering* (which, with cognate words, occurs 16 times). The word *hope* is tied to it—the Christian hope in the time of trial.

OUTLINE:

I. **Suffering and the security of believers produces joy,** Chapter 1:1-9

II. **Suffering and the Scriptures produces holiness,** Chapter 1:10-25

III. **Suffering and the suffering of Christ,** Chapters 2–4

  A. Produces separation, Chapter 2

  B. Produces Christian conduct, Chapter 3

    1. Conduct in the home, vv. 1-7

    2. Conduct in the church, vv. 8-17

    3. Christ's suffering preached by the Spirit in Noah's day, vv. 18-22

  C. Produces obedience to the will of God, Chapter 4

IV. **Suffering and the Second Coming of Christ,** Chapter 5

  A. Produces service and hope, vv. 1-4

  B. Produces humility and patience, vv. 5-14

2 Peter

2 Peter

WRITER: Simon Peter (2 Peter 1:1). The Petrine authorship of 2 Peter has been challenged more than the authorship of any other book in the New Testament. Dr. William Moorehead said, "The Second Epistle of Peter comes to us with less historical support of its genuineness than any other book of the New Testament." However, this has caused conservative scholars to give adequate attention to this epistle so that today it is well established that Peter wrote this letter. The autobiographical sections afford internal evidence of the Petrine authorship (see 2 Peter 1:13, 14, 16-18; 3:1).

DATE: About A.D. 66. This second epistle was written shortly after his first epistle (2 Peter 3:1) and a short while before his martyrdom (1:13, 14). (See 1 Peter.)

THEME: This is the swan song of Peter, as 2 Timothy is the swan song of Paul. There is a striking similarity. Both epistles put up a warning sign, along the pilgrim pathway the church is traveling, to identify the awful apostasy that was on the way at that time and now in our time has arrived. What was then like a cloud the size of a man's hand today envelops the sky and produces a storm of hurricane proportions. Peter warns of heresy among teachers as Paul warns of heresy among the laity. Both Peter and Paul speak in a joyful manner of their approaching death (2 Peter 1:13, 14; 2 Timothy 4:6-8). Both apostles anchor the church on the Scriptures as the only defense against the coming storm.

The similarity of 2 Peter to Paul's last epistle of 2 Timothy explains the sharp contrast between Peter's first and second letters. The subject has changed, and the difference is as great as that which exists between Paul's letters to the Romans and to Timothy.

Nevertheless, the theme is explained on the basis of the words which Peter uses here as contrasted to his first epistle. The words are different, with the exception of the word *precious*, which occurs in this epistle twice in the first chapter. Likewise, the word *faith* occurs twice in the first chapter.

The characteristic word is *knowledge* (occurring 16 times with cognate words). The epitome of the epistle is expressed in the injunction contained in 2 Peter 3:18, the final verse.

True Gnosticism is not some esoteric information concerning a formula, a rite, or ritual; nor is it some secret order or password. It is to know Jesus Christ as He is revealed to man in the Word of God. This is the secret of life and of Christian living (see John 17:3).

OUTLINE:

I.   **Addition of Christian graces gives assurance,** Chapter 1:1-14
     "The [full] knowledge of God, and of Jesus, our Lord" is the foundation on which Christian character is built (see v. 2).

II. **Authority of the Scriptures attested by fulfilled prophecy,** Chapter 1:15-21
     Scriptures give light for obedience in dark days.

III. **Apostasy brought in by false teachers,** Chapter 2
     Church should beware of false teachers and not false prophets.

IV. **Attitude toward return of the Lord is a test of apostates,** Chapter 3:1-4

V.   **Agenda of God for the world,** Chapter 3:5-13

   A. Past world, vv. 5, 6

   B. Present world, vv. 7-12

   C. Future world, v. 13

VI. **Admonition to believers,** Chapter 3:14-18
     Knowledge of God's program is an incentive to grow in the knowledge of our Lord and Savior Jesus Christ.

1 John

1 John

WRITER: John the Apostle

DATE: A.D. 90-100. John evidently wrote his Gospel first, then his epistles, and finally the book of Revelation before his death about A.D. 100.

PURPOSE: John expressed the purpose for his writing in each of the three types of revelation:

His *Gospel* in John 20:30, 31
His first *epistle* in 1 John 5:13
His *revelation* in Revelation 1:19

Actually, there is a fivefold purpose expressed in 1 John:

1 John 1:3	"That ye also may have fellowship with us [other believers]: and truly our fellowship is with the Father, and with his Son Jesus Christ."
1 John 1:4	"That your joy may be full."
1 John 2:1	"That ye sin not."
1 John 5:13	"That ye may know that ye have eternal life."
1 John 5:13	"That ye may believe on the name of the Son of God."

THE FAMILY OF GOD: This epistle has been called the *sanctum sanctorum* of the New Testament. It takes the child of God across the threshold into the fellowship of the Father's home. It is the *family* epistle; John is writing here to the family of God. *Father* is used 13 times and *little children* 11 times. Paul wrote to the church; John wrote to the family. The church is a body of believers in the position where we are blessed "with all spiritual blessings in heavenly places in Christ" (Ephesians 1:3). We are given that position when we believe on the Lord Jesus Christ. In the family we have a relationship which can be broken, but is restored when "we confess our sins." Then He "is faithful and just to forgive us our sins, and to cleanse us from all unrighteousness" (1 John 1:9).

The body of believers who constitute the church are in the family of God, though the family is larger than the church. The church and the family are both in the Kingdom of God but are not synonymous terms.

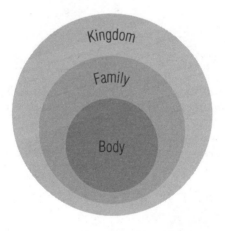

KEY WORDS: "Light" (used six times); "love" (used 33 times); "life" (used 15 times); "fellowship" (used four times); know (used 38 times)—John wrote to meet the first heresy that entered the church. It was Gnosticism, which boasted super-knowledge. It accepted the deity of Jesus, but it denied His humanity. John gives us the true Gnosticism—knowledge.

OUTLINE:

I.   God is LIGHT (1:5), Chapters 1:1–2:2

A. Prologue, Chapter 1:1, 2

B. How the little children may have fellowship with God, Chapters 1:3–2:2

   1. By walking in light, 1:3-7

   2. By confessing sin, 1:8-10

   3. By advocacy of Christ, 2:1, 2

II.   God is LOVE (4:8), Chapters 2:3–4:21

A. How the dear children may have fellowship with each other by walking in love, Chapter 2:3-14

B. The dear children must not love the world, Chapter 2:15-28

C. How the dear children may know each other and live together, Chapters 2:29–4:21

   1. The Father's love for His children, 2:29—3:3

   2. The two natures of the believer in action, 3:4-24

   3. Warning against false teachers, 4:1-6

   4. God is love; little children will love each other, 4:7-21

III.   God is LIFE (5:12), Chapter 5

A. Victory over the world, vv. 1-5

B. Assurance of salvation, vv. 6-21

2 John

2 John

WRITER: John the Apostle

DATE: A.D. 90—100

PERSONAL LETTER: This epistle is like Philemon in that it is a personal letter written by John to "the elect lady." Is the Greek word *electa* a title, or does it refer to a Christian lady in the early church by the name of Electa? It would seem that it was addressed to some lady in the church or to a local church that was extending hospitality to all those who claimed to be Christian, though some were heretics. John warns against entertaining such.

THEME: For truth's sake. Truth is worth contending for, and it is wrong to receive false teachers.

OUTLINE:

I.   **Love expressed in the boundary of truth,** vv. 1–6
   "Love in truth"

II.   **Life is an expression of the doctrine of Christ,** vv. 7–11
   (False doctrine leads to evil deeds.)

III.   **Personal greeting,** vv. 12, 13
   (False teachers are not to be received by the Christian, but true teachers are to be received with joy.)

3 John

3 John

WRITER: John the Apostle

DATE: A.D. 90—100

PERSONALITIES: This is a letter similar to John's second epistle, in that it is personal in character, and it carries the same theme of *truth*. However, this letter deals with personalities, which will be noted in the outline. In his second epistle, John says that *truth* is worth standing for; in the third epistle that *truth* is worth working for.

OUTLINE:

I. **Gaius, beloved brother in the early church, vv. 1—8**
   (Gaius, the one to whom the letter is addressed, is urged to extend hospitality to true teachers of the Word.)

II. **Diotrephes, "who loveth to have the pre-eminence," vv. 9—11**
   (Evil deeds are an expression of false doctrine.)

III. **Demetrius "hath good report of all men, and of the truth itself," vv. 12—14**
   (A good life is an expression of true doctrine.)

Jude

Jude

WRITER: Judas. Jude (this is the English form of the name Judas) was the brother of James (see notes on Epistle of James) and was also a half-brother of the Lord Jesus Christ (Matthew 13:55).

DATE: A.D. 66-69

THEME: Assurance in days of apostasy. The word for "keep" occurs five times (see verses 1, 6, 21, 24).

REMARKS: Jude was intending to write an epistle regarding our "common salvation" when the Spirit detoured him to write concerning the apostasy. It is a graphic and striking description of the apostasy. What was a little cloud the size of a man's hand in Jude's day is, in our day, a storm of hurricane proportions—because we are in the apostasy of which he foretold. It is a question now of how much worse it can become before genuine believers are taken out by the Rapture.

Jude gives the only record in the Scriptures of the contention over the body of Moses. Also, only Jude gives the prophecy of Enoch.

Jude affords a fitting introduction to the book of Revelation.

OUTLINE:

I.   OCCASION of the epistle, v. 1-3

   A. Assurance for believers, vv. 1, 2
      (Sanctified, kept, called)

   B. Change of theme to apostasy, v. 3

II.   OCCURRENCES of apostasy, vv. 4-16

   A. Inception of apostasy, v. 4

   B. Israel in wilderness in unbelief destroyed, v. 5

   C. Angels rebelled; kept in chains, v. 6

   D. Sodom and Gomorrah sinned in sensuality; destroyed by fire, v. 7

   E. Modern apostate teachers identified, vv. 8-10
      (Despise authority)

   F. Cain, Balaam, and Korah are examples of apostates, v. 11

   G. Modern apostate teachers defined and described, vv. 12-16

III.   OCCUPATION of believers in days of apostasy, vv. 17-25

   A. Believers warned by apostles that these apostates would come, vv. 17-19

   B. What believers must do in days of apostasy, vv. 20-25

Revelation

Revelation

WRITER: John the apostle

DATE: About A.D. 95

STRIKING FEATURES:

- It is the only prophetic book in the New Testament (in contrast to 17 prophetic books in the Old Testament).
- John, the writer, reaches farther back into eternity past than any other writer in Scripture (John 1:1-3). He reaches farther on into eternity future in the book of Revelation.
- Special blessing is promised the readers of this book (Revelation 1:3). Likewise, a warning is issued to those who tamper with its contents (Revelation 22:18, 19).
- Revelation is not a sealed book (Revelation 22:10). Contrast Daniel 12:9. It is a revelation (apocalypse), which is an unveiling.
- It is a series of visions, expressed in symbols.
- This book is like a great Union Station where the great trunk lines of prophecy come in from other portions of Scripture. Revelation does not originate but consummates. It is imperative to a right understanding of the book to be able to trace each great subject of prophecy from the first reference to the terminal.

At least ten great subjects of prophecy find their consummation here:

1 – The Lord Jesus Christ (Genesis 3:15)

2 – The church (Matthew 16:18)

3 – The resurrection and translation of saints
(1 Thessalonians 4:13-18; 1 Corinthians 15:51, 52)

4 – The Great Tribulation (Deuteronomy 4:30, 31)

5 – Satan and evil (Ezekiel 28:11-18)

6 – The "man of sin" (Ezekiel 28:1-10)

7 – The course and end of apostate Christendom (Daniel 2:31-45; Matthew 13)

8 – The beginning, course, and end of the "times of the Gentiles" (Daniel 2:37; Luke 1:24)

9 – The second coming of Christ (Jude 14, 15)

10 – Israel's covenants (Genesis 12:1-3), five things promised Israel

KEY VERSES: Revelation 1:18, 19

OUTLINE:

I.   **The PERSON of Jesus Christ—Christ in glory,** Chapter 1

A. Title of the book, v. 1

B. Method of revelation, v. 2

C. Beatitude of Bible study, v. 3

D. Greetings from John the writer, and from Jesus Christ in heaven, vv. 4-8

E. The post-incarnate Christ in a glorified body, judging His church
(the great High Priest in the Holy of Holies), vv. 9-18

F. Time division of the contents of the apocalypse, v. 19

G. Interpretation of the seven stars and seven lampstands, v. 20

II. **The POSSESSION of Jesus Christ—the church in the world,**
Chapters 2, 3

A. Letter of Christ to the church in Ephesus, Chapter 2:1-7

B. Letter of Christ to the church in Smyrna, Chapter 2:8-11

C. Letter of Christ to the church in Pergamum, Chapter 2:12-17

D. Letter of Christ to the church in Thyatira, Chapter 2:18-29

E. Letter of Christ to the church in Sardis, Chapter 3:1-6

F. Letter of Christ to the church in Philadelphia, Chapter 3:7-13

G. Letter of Christ to the church in Laodicea, Chapter 3:14-22

III. **The PROGRAM of Jesus Christ—the scene in heaven,** Chapters 4–22

A. The church in heaven with Christ, Chapters 4, 5
... I will come again, and receive you unto myself; that where I am, there ye may be also. (John 14:3)

1. Throne of God, 4:1-3

2. 24 elders, 4:4, 5

3. Four living creatures, 4:6-11

4. Book with seven seals, 5:1-4

5. Christ: the Lion of the tribe of Judah and the Lamb that has been slain, 5:5-10

6. A myriad of angels of heaven joins the song of praise and redemption, 5:11, 12

7. Universal worship of the Savior and Sovereign of the universe, 5:13, 14

B. The Great Tribulation in the world, Chapters 6–18

1. Opening of the seven-sealed book, Chapters 6—8:1

a. **Opening of the first seal,** 6:1, 2
(Rider on a white horse)

b. **Opening of the second seal,** 6:3, 4
(Rider on a red horse)

c. **Opening of the third seal,** 6:5, 6
(Rider on a black horse)

d. **Opening of the fourth seal,** 6:7, 8
(Rider on a pale horse)

e. **Opening of the fifth seal,** 6:9-11
(Prayer of the martyred remnant)

f. **Opening of the sixth seal,** 6:12-17
(The Day of Wrath has come—beginning of the last half of the Great Tribulation)

g. Interlude, Chapter 7

    i. Reason for the interlude between the sixth and seventh seals, vv. 1-3

    ii. Remnant of Israel sealed, vv. 4-8

    iii. Redeemed multitude of Gentiles, vv. 9-17

h. Opening of the seventh seal, 8:1
(Introduction of seven trumpets)

2. Blowing of the **seven trumpets**, Chapters 8:2—11:19

a. Angel at the altar with censer of incense, 8:2-6

b. First trumpet—trees burnt, 8:7

c. Second trumpet—seas become blood, 8:8, 9

d. Third trumpet—fresh water becomes bitter, 8:10, 11

e. Fourth trumpet—sun, moon, stars smitten, 8:12, 13

f. Fifth trumpet—fallen star and plague of locusts, 9:1-12

g. Sixth trumpet—angels loosed at river Euphrates, 9:13-21

h. Interlude between the sixth and seventh trumpets, 10:1–11:14

    i. The strong angel with the little book, 10:1-7

    ii. John eats the little book, 10:8-11

    iii. Date for the ending of "the times of the Gentiles," 11:1, 2

    iv. Duration of the prophesying of the two witnesses, 11:3-12

    v. Doom of the second woe—great earthquake, 11:13, 14

i. Seventh trumpet—end of Great Tribulation and opening of temple in heaven, 11:15-19

3. **Seven performers** during the Great Tribulation, Chapters 12, 13

a. The woman—Israel, 12:1, 2

b. The red dragon—Satan, 12:3, 4

c. The child of the woman—Jesus Christ, 12:5, 6

d. Michael, the archangel, wars with the dragon, 12:7-12

e. The dragon persecutes the woman, 12:13-16

f. Remnant of Israel, 12:17

g. Wild beast out of the sea—a political power and a person, 13:1-10

    i. Wild beast, description, vv. 1, 2

    ii. Wild beast, death-dealing stroke, v. 3

    iii. Wild beast, deity assumed, vv. 4, 5

    iv. Wild beast, defying God, vv. 6-8

    v. Wild beast, defiance denied to anyone, vv. 9, 10

h. Wild beast out of the earth—a religious leader, 13:11-18

    i. Wild beast, description, v. 11

    ii. Wild beast, delegated authority, vv. 12-14

    iii. Wild beast, delusion perpetrated on the world, vv. 15-17

    iv. Wild beast, designation, v. 18

4. Looking to the **end of the Great Tribulation**, Chapter 14

a. Picture of the lamb with the 144,000, vv. 1-5

b. Proclamation of the everlasting gospel, vv. 6, 7

c. Pronouncement of judgment on Babylon, v. 8

d. Pronouncement of judgment on those who received mark of the beast, vv. 9-12

e. Praise for those who die in the Lord, v. 13

f. Preview of Armageddon, vv. 14-20

5. Pouring out of the **seven mixing bowls of wrath**, Chapters 15, 16

a. Preparation for final judgment of the Great Tribulation, 15:1–16:1

    i. Tribulation saints in heaven worship God because He is holy and just, 15:1-4

    ii. Temple of the tabernacle opened in heaven that seven angels, having seven golden bowls, might proceed forth, 15:5–16:1

b. Pouring out of the first bowl, 16:2

c. Pouring out of the second bowl, 16:3

d. Pouring out of the third bowl, 16:4-7

e. Pouring out of the fourth bowl, 16:8, 9

f. Pouring out of the fifth bowl, 16:10, 11

g. Pouring out of the sixth bowl, 16:12

h. Interlude: kings of inhabited earth proceed to Har-Magedon, 16:13-16

i. Pouring out of the seventh bowl, 16:17-21

6. The **two Babylons judged**, Chapters 17, 18

  a. The apostate church in the Great Tribulation, Chapter 17

   i. Great harlot riding the wild beast, vv. 1-7

   ii. Wild beast destroys the great harlot, vv. 8-18

  b. Political and commercial Babylon judged, Chapter 18

   i. Announcement of fall of commercial and political Babylon, vv. 1-8

   ii. Anguish in the world because of Babylon's judgment, vv. 9-19

   iii. Anticipation of joy in heaven because of judgment on Babylon, vv. 20-24

C. Marriage of the Lamb and return of Christ in judgment, Chapter 19

 1. Four hallelujahs, vv. 1-6

 2. Bride of the Lamb and marriage supper, vv. 7-10

 3. Return of Christ as King of kings and Lord of lords, vv. 11-16

 4. War of Armageddon, vv. 17, 18

 5. Hell opened, vv. 19-21

D. Millennium, Chapter 20

 1. Satan bound 1000 years, vv. 1-3

 2. Saints of the Great Tribulation reign with Christ 1000 years, vv. 4-6

 3. Satan loosed after 1000 years, vv. 7-9

 4. Satan cast into lake of fire and brimstone, v. 10

 5. Setting of Great White Throne where lost are judged and follow Satan into lake of fire and brimstone, vv. 11-15

E. Entrance into eternity; eternity unveiled, Chapters 21, 22

 1. New heaven, new earth, New Jerusalem, 21:1, 2

 2. New era, 21:3-8

 3. New Jerusalem, description of the eternal abode of the bride, 21:9-21

4. New relationship—God dwelling with man, 21:22, 23

5. New center of the new creation, 21:24-27

6. River of the water of life and tree of life, 22:1-5

7. Promise of return of Christ, 22:6-16

8. Final invitation and warning, 22:17-19

9. Final promise and prayer, 22:20, 21

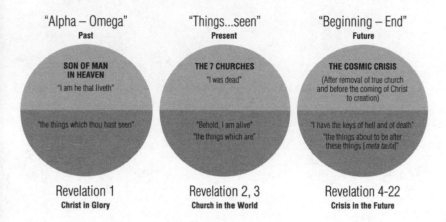

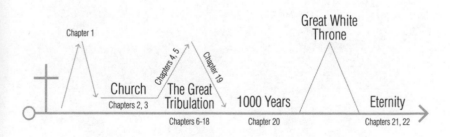

ABOUT *THRU THE BIBLE*

At the core of what THRU the BIBLE is and what we do, is the conviction that the Bible is true and trustworthy. We believe God uses His Word uniquely in each of our lives to transform the way we think, believe, and live.

How does He do this? We believe that, in part, He does this by telling us His own story: The story of His love, His redemption—a story that He planned and put into place before our time began. At its heart, it's the story of how He has opened the way for us to know Him, to love and obey Him, to grow deeper day by day in the ways we trust Him. It's a beautiful story that gets better every time we hear it.

It's the story THRU the BIBLE tells every day on the air and invites people to listen.

Dr. J. Vernon McGee, our founder and teacher, loved to tell the story more than anything else in the world. He began teaching on the radio in 1941, hoping that the San Gabriel Valley and the metropolitan Los Angeles area would pay attention and respond to the wonders of the Bible, simply told.

And to his surprise, people listened. Because not only is the Bible a good story, and Dr. McGee a good storyteller, but through the Bible is also the primary way God draws us to Himself.

While teaching in the book of Hebrews, Dr. McGee said,

> *"The only way you and I are going to stay close to Jesus is to stay close to His Word ... that's why we're spending time in the Word of God, and the reason I read letters from people on the air. They say 'for the first time I found out about the joy of the Lord.' The Christian life has been a yoke on them; all they knew was duty and discipline. But when you spend time studying the Bible, you can't help but be drawn to the Person of Jesus. That's what you should listen for in the letters we read—listen for the joy of walking close to Jesus."*

That's why it is not unusual for there to be many longtime, repeat travelers on "The Bible Bus," as Dr. McGee calls the journey we take through the Word every five years. People come aboard and stay aboard because they grow closer to Jesus with each trip. And the good news is, there's always room for more on the Bible Bus. So invite your friends.

But we must be clear: People don't come aboard because of Dr. McGee. They come because Dr. McGee points them to Jesus. No one would be more surprised than J. Vernon McGee at the worldwide response to his country preaching, with simple ways and endearing mannerisms. Yes, we honor his courage to answer the call, but we give the glory to God for the generations of lives changed. And we'll keep telling those stories until Jesus comes again.

We hope that in telling our story, we're really telling your story ... about the joy you found in walking closer to Jesus ... about the gratitude you feel for that window of understanding into His Word ... for the first time you heard the name of Jesus and knew it was Him who you've been looking for all along. We are privileged to hear these same stories every day, coming from nearly every nation on earth.

Yes, that's how far God has taken this simple story—to nearly every nation on earth in over 200 languages. This stunning fact alone testifies to the surpassing power of God at work, using simple jars of clay (see 2 Corinthians 4:7).

The THRU the BIBLE story is simple ... and deep. Just like yours. It's a story of God reaching down to man—and man, reaching back. We'll be telling these stories to each other throughout eternity, so you won't mind if we get in good practice now.

We love to tell the Bible's story ... the story of Jesus and His love. Join us on the Bible Bus today to hear it again in a new way. We're saving you a seat.

TTB.ORG